Antonius Piip, Zigfrīds Meierovics and
Augustinas Voldemaras

Makers
of the
Modern
World

Antonius Piip, Zigfrīds Meierovics and Augustinas Voldemaras
The Baltic States
Charlotte Alston

HAUS HISTORIES

First published in Great Britain in 2010 by
Haus Publishing Ltd
70 Cadogan Place
London SW1X 9AH
www.hauspublishing.com

A CIP catalogue record for this book
is available from the British Library

ISBN 978-1-905791-71-2

Series design by Susan Buchanan
Typeset in Sabon by MacGuru Ltd
Printed in Dubai by Oriental Press
Map by Martin Lubikowski, ML Design, London

Contents

Introduction

The collapse of the Austro-Hungarian, Russian and Ottoman Empires at the end of the First World War threw up all sorts of new territorial issues in areas unfamiliar to Western diplomats. When the British Prime Minister David Lloyd George admitted in the House of Commons in April 1919 that he had 'never heard of' Teschen, an uproar ensued.[1] While the Austro-Hungarian Empire broke into its component parts, revolution in Russia brought about the secession of a number of states around the Empire's borders. Many did not survive the early 1920s as independent states – Ukraine, Belarus, Georgia, Armenia and Azerbaijan. The three Baltic States (Estonia, Latvia and Lithuania), along with Finland and Poland, were among those that did achieve independence and Western recognition. They generated their own 'Teschen incidents' in the struggle by Western diplomats to get to grips with Baltic affairs. The story of the French military mission in Latvia arriving with a supply of Yen to finance its trip as those responsible had assumed Latvia to be a Japanese island may be apocryphal, but it expresses the confusion of Western officials well.[2]

The position of the Estonian, Latvian and Lithuanian governments was perilous in 1919. They faced German, Russian

1

and Polish occupation of territory they claimed. All three countries sent delegations to the Paris Peace Conference, to seek assistance and recognition from the victorious Allied powers. The three men at the centre of this book each represented their country at the Conference. Augustinas Voldemaras, a controversial politician with a quick temper and 'a peculiar knack of antagonising people',[3] was Prime Minister of Lithuania until he left the country in December 1918 to seek external support for the cause of Lithuanian independence. He led the Lithuanian delegation at the Conference, and played an important role in his country's inter-war history, serving as Prime Minister under the authoritarian presidency of Antanas Smetona from 1926. Zigfrīds Meierovics was the Latvian Foreign Minister, in the government led by Kārlis Ulmanis, and he represented his country at the Peace Conference in that capacity. A quiet and statesmanlike man, he was in many ways the architect of the policy of Baltic co-operation and served as Latvian Foreign Minister almost continuously, and as Prime Minister twice, before his untimely death in 1925. Estonian diplomacy in Paris was conducted very much as a team effort, with each member of the delegation making a unique contribution. This study will focus on the work of Antonius (Ants) Piip, the Estonian representative in London and the 'fundamental strategist of the Estonian campaign' in Paris.[4] Piip was a professor of international law and a member of the government headed by Konstantin Päts, in which Jaan Poska, the nominal head of the Paris delegation, was Foreign Minister. Piip had good relations with Meierovics and with the British delegation, who were certainly the most sympathetic of the Allies to the Baltic cause. Piip served as Prime Minister and State Elder of Estonia in 1920–1 and repeatedly as Foreign Minister in the period 1921–40.

Baltic independence was only possible because both Germany and Russia were defeated in the First World War. While the Baltic States' geographical position between these two powers caused them many difficulties, it also created opportunities in an international forum like the Paris Peace Conference. 'Being a young and untried diplomat was a heady thing in an Eastern Europe from which Germany and Russia seemed excluded.'[5] Outside the official structures of the Peace Conference, there were numerous opportunities for networking and lobbying. Some of the better negotiators – the Greek Prime Minister Eleftherios Venizelos or the Czech Foreign Minister Eduard Beneš for example – significantly furthered their country's cause by their diplomatic skills. On a lesser scale, effective lobbying at the Peace Conference enabled the Baltic diplomats to raise the profile of their countries, even if they did not achieve immediate recognition. Exploiting Western diplomats' desire to support anti-Bolshevik and anti-German elements on the fringes of Russia, and playing on the Wilsonian rhetoric of national self-determination, they were able to convert support at the Conference into recognition of their independence once the Russian Civil War was over.

While issues concerning the states around Russia's borders were much discussed at the Paris Peace Conference, few were settled there. Arguably other post-war peace treaties did more to determine the future status of the Baltic States – the Treaty of Brest-Litovsk in 1918; the Treaties of Tartu, Riga and Moscow in 1920; and the Polish-Soviet Peace of 1921. What the Paris Peace Conference did was provide the opportunity for Baltic diplomats to internationalise their cause and to create the image of a coherent regional identity. In these respects the work of Ants Piip, Zigfrīds Meierovics and Augustinas Voldemaras was crucial.

Antonius (Ants) Piip (1884–1942).

I
The Lives and the Land

1

A Brief History

Estonia, Latvia and Lithuania lie on the eastern Baltic seaboard, between two of the 19th and 20th century's greatest powers, Germany and Russia, and two major powers of earlier centuries, Sweden and Poland. Their history is characterised by the overlapping influence of these dominant and invasive polities. In the 20th century these three small states shared a common trajectory – escape from the Russian Empire, inter-war independence, wartime occupation, reabsorption by the Soviet Union, and renewed struggle for independence at the end of the century. They were treated as a bloc in the policies of the larger powers, and attempted to build regional alliances in the interests of their own collective security. This common fate masks the very different experiences of these states before the 20th century. The peoples and the territory of Estonia, Latvia and Lithuania differ from each other historically in terms of language, culture and religion. There are fundamental differences even between the Estonians and Latvians, while 'almost every historical generalisation that can be made about the Latvians and Estonians has to be modified to take account of the Lithuanians'.[1] Even in the early 20th century any attempt to include Lithuania along with Estonia and Latvia in a survey of the 'Baltic states' was regarded as to some extent arbitrary.[2]

The native inhabitants of Estonia, Latvia and Lithuania are descended from tribes who settled on the eastern Baltic shore as long as 4,000 years ago. Tribes speaking Finno-Ugric languages setled north of the Vaina River; they had moved there from the Volga region of Russia. Indo-European peoples, including Couronians, Zemgalians and Latgalians settled to the south. Tacitus, writing in the 1st century AD, refers to the people of this region as 'Aesti' – collectors of amber and energetic cultivators of crops.[3] Modern Estonian belongs to the Finno-Ugric language group, is closely related to Finnish and more distantly related to Hungarian. A language close to Estonian is also spoken by the Livs, a distinct ethnic group in north-west Latvia of whom only around a thousand remain. Modern Latvian and Lithuanian are Indo-European languages. Lithuanian received a great deal of attention from mid-19th century philologists as a result of the discovery that it was the closest living language to Sanskrit.[4]

Geographical location differentiated the Baltic peoples in terms of trade and therefore economic development. The Lithuanians were isolated from the sea and the Nemunas River only skirted their territory to the north. In contrast, the Daugava River and viable ports on the Baltic coast meant that the Estonians and Latvians engaged actively in trade, trafficking amber to the Romans and furs to the German tribes, in exchange for metal goods, salt and textiles.

Their geographical position also exposed the Baltic peoples to the attentions of foreign powers. In the 12th century the threat was a continuation of the Viking expansion, now focused through the Kingdoms of Denmark and Sweden. In the 13th century, German merchants, missionaries and Crusaders established extensive bridgeheads in the eastern Baltic. Tied into the north German Hanseatic League, these bridgeheads turned into an enduring colonial complex of trading cities, bishops who were often territorial princes, and religious and military orders like the Sword Brethren, the Livonian Order, and most famously the Teutonic Knights.

This medieval colonisation engulfed almost the whole southern and eastern Baltic coast from Lübeck to Narva: only the Lithuanians escaped conquest and Christianisation. During the 13th century they acquired political coherence, notably under Grand Duke Mindaugas (1236–63). Not only did they hold off the Teutonic Knights, they expanded into the ruined Russian principalities as the power of their Tatar overlords declined. Under Grand Prince Gediminas (1316–41) Vilnius became Lithuania's capital, a commercial centre with a large Jewish, as well as Lithuanian, population. Vilnius remained notorious for its international character – Johann David Wunderer, a late 16th-century visitor, claimed it would be difficult to find 'a place in Christianity where more strange nations and more unusual clothes come together'.[5] By the late 14th century, the Grand Duchy extended from the Baltic to the Black Sea, taking in much of modern-day Ukraine and Belarus. In 1386 Grand Duke Jogaila married Jadwiga, child Queen of Poland, with far-reaching consequences. The ideological basis of the Crusader threat was removed as the Lithuanians began to Christianise more or less on their own terms – or at least those of the ruling prince – and Jogaila's dynasty became one of the great powers of medieval Christendom. The much more institutionally developed Kingdom of Poland introduced new forms of administration into Lithuania. In the 15th century, Poland-Lithuania contained and then neutralised the German Crusader threat in the north. The price for the Lithuanians was not only Christianisation, but also Polonisation: its nobility were becoming Polish in customs, manners and language long before the formal union of the Polish-Lithuanian Commonwealth in 1569.

The German Crusader states on the Baltic from Danzig to Narva stabilised, and then with the coming of the Reformation went Lutheran and secularised themselves as principalities. In the 1530s aristocratic warrior monks became a territorial nobility – but remained a German elite dominating largely non-German peasant societies. Their grip was strong enough to repulse Tsar Ivan the Terrible's attempts to conquer the Baltic coast between 1558 and 1584, but their independence did not survive the attentions of the Danes and Swedes from the mid-16th century. In the early 17th century the Swedes established themselves on the Baltic littoral, despite local resistance and Polish and Danish competition. They went on to occupy many Prussian and north German cities and to intervene militarily deep inside Germany. Swedish dominance in the Baltic beat off all challengers until it eventually collapsed during the Great Northern War with Russia in 1700–21.

The Treaty of Nystad in 1721 formalised Russia's breakthrough to the Baltic. Peter the Great incorporated Estonia and Livonia, Ingria and Karelia. With Sweden in retreat, there was no other great power to bar the rise of Russia in the region: Poland-Lithuania's bankrupt elective monarchy made it an ineffective and incoherent polity, increasingly vulnerable to predatory neighbours. Prussia, Russia and Austria-Hungary combined against her in the Partition of 1772. When internal reforms looked as though they might succeed, the further Partitions of 1793 and 1795 eliminated the Polish-Lithuanian Commonwealth completely. Russia absorbed the Duchy of Courland and most of Lithuania in 1795. Its grip on the eastern Baltic coast was complete.

2

The Baltic Region and the Russian Empire

Great variations in the social, economic, cultural and religious makeup of the Baltic region persisted under Russian rule. Peter the Great confirmed the dominant position of the Baltic German nobility and of the Lutheran Church in Estonia and Livonia shortly after the signature of the Treaty of Nystad in August 1721. The German nobility owned the land, and German merchant elites dominated trade. Administration and education in the region were conducted in German. The Baltic Germans came to be valued by Peter the Great as loyal and effective administrators and over time gained positions in the central bureaucracy of the Russian Empire and in the Russian army. It was therefore not surprising that the Baltic Germans also remained dominant in Courland after its absorption in 1795. In Lithuania the Polonised aristocracy and the Roman Catholic Church retained their position, although the Russian government treated them with greater suspicion. The Russian period therefore saw a reinforcement of the division between the Baltic provinces – Estonia, Livonia and Courland – and the Polish-Lithuanian provinces, of which by the mid-19th century Vilnius, Kaunas, Grodno and Suwalki contained the bulk of the Lithuanian population.

Under the influence of 'enlightened' German landowners striving for agricultural efficiency and looking also to secure their own position in the region, serfdom was abolished in Estonia in 1816, in Courland in 1817 and in Livonia in 1819. This was 40 years ahead of emancipation in Lithuania and the rest of the Russian Empire, but the restrictions on movement and the purchase of land that accompanied this emancipation limited any further alterations to the traditional social structure. There were educational opportunities for Latvians and Estonians, but those that took advantage of them tended to rise into the local elites and become Germanised. When nationalist movements emerged in the 19th century, they therefore focused on the need for national languages to transcend class and status boundaries. During the course of the 19th century local Russian authorities became aware of the dangers of having native inhabitants of these areas educated in German, rather than Russian, especially after the unification of Germany. At the same time they were becoming more confident in their ability to roll out Russian administrative models and culture across the Empire, freeing them from reliance on traditional elites to govern in the borderlands. The policies of 'Russification' that were applied both in the Baltic and Polish-Lithuanian provinces were therefore targeted initially at the dominant elites (Germans and Poles) rather than the nascent native national movements (Estonian, Latvian and Lithuanian). For parallel reasons these national movements developed in opposition to German and Polish domination, but not necessarily in opposition to a Russian Empire which seemed to share an interest in eroding traditional power structures in the region.

These developments gave native Estonians, Latvians and Lithuanians opportunities they might not have had a generation earlier. This is illustrated by the early careers of the three protagonists of this book, Augustinas Voldemaras, Ants Piip and Zigfrīds Meierovics. All were born in the 1880s. None came in any sense from the traditional landowning or mercantile elites. All originated in small towns or rural society. Two were academic high achievers who transcended provincial origins to study in St Petersburg and then abroad, and the other might have done so but for his difficult family circumstances.

Augustinas Voldemaras, who was born in 1883 in the Vilnius district in eastern Lithuania, did not come from a wealthy or well-educated family – his father was a small farmer – but he was able to attend the University of St Petersburg, where he studied history and philosophy to Masters level, receiving his Masters Degree in 1910. The gold medals he received for both his undergraduate and Masters work meant that he was awarded a scholarship for Doctoral study at the university.[1] He studied in Italy and Sweden before joining the faculty of the University of St Petersburg, as a Lecturer in History, in 1915.

Ants Piip was born in 1884 in Tuhalaane, in Estonia, also the son of a small independent farmer. He studied at a teaching college in Kuldīga (Goldigen) in Latvia, and at Kuressaare State High School. He went on to study law at St Petersburg University between 1908 and 1913, and held a variety of teaching and administrative posts in Alūksne (Alulinn, Marienburg), Kuressaare and St Petersburg. He held a research scholarship at St Petersburg University between 1913 and 1916, but also worked for the Russian government, first in the Ministry of Justice and then in the Ministry of the

Interior. Like Voldemaras, Piip also spent time outside the Russian Empire, studying briefly at Berlin University in 1912.

Zigfrīds Meierovics was a few years younger, being born in 1887 in Durben near Liepāja (Libau). Although he was born into a 'Germanised' Latvian family, his educational opportunities were more limited than those of Piip and Voldemaras. Meierovics' mother died in childbirth, and his father, a converted Jewish doctor, suffered from mental illness. From a young age Meierovics was brought up by his mother's brother, who was a schoolteacher in Sabile in western Latvia. He was educated at the Riga Polytechnic Institute, and forged a career for himself in agrarian banking.[2] He appears to have been the only one of the three not to have left the Russian Empire before the Revolution.

By the turn of the century, all three men would become involved in their countries' nationalist movements. These emerged from the 1860s, and like most other European national movements, revolved initially around the rediscovery and promotion of native languages and folklore. This led to the publication of newspapers, the establishment of nationalist societies and song festivals (forms which would re-emerge in the late 1980s and early 1990s). As the movements developed, so did many of the ideas which would provide foundations for more overtly political rhetoric concerning autonomy and independence in the early 20th century.

From the 1860s onwards more public use began to be made of the terms 'Estonia' and 'Estonian', 'Latvia' and 'Latvian'. J V Jannsen's newspaper *Eesti Postimees* (The Estonian Courier) for example was one of the first publications to address its readers as Estonians.[3] A group of Latvians at the University of Dorpat (Tartu), the only higher education institution in the Baltic provinces and very Baltic

German in character, called themselves the 'Young Latvians' in imitation of the Young Italy and Young Germany movements.[4] The Riga Latvian Association, founded in 1868, promoted Latvian language and culture. It was still going strong in the 1910s when Zigfrīds Meierovics was a member. A market for Baltic language publications developed, helped by the exceptionally high literacy rate – over 90 per cent in Estonia and Livonia in comparison to 30 per cent in other parts of the Russian Empire – and by the growth of the cities.[5] Riga is a particularly notable example: as Latvians flocked there from the countryside they created a market for Latvian theatre, art and publications. There was an increase in interest in national folklore – the Estonian epic *Kalevipoeg*, compiled by Friedrich Reinhold Kreutzwald on the model of the Finnish *Kalevala*, was published in 1857–61. Baltic history was reinterpreted in the light of nationalist ideology, with the era before German colonisation and the advent of Christianity being presented as an era of flourishing national culture and ideals. The conquest and colonisation of the region by Baltic German overlords, in contrast, was a period of darkness and serfdom which still continued. Only when free nations were born in which Estonians and Latvians reclaimed their land would a new age arrive. All of these motifs are present, for example, in Andrejs Pumpurs' Latvian national epic, *The Bearslayer*, written in 1888. Much of this rhetoric was directed against the Baltic German elites, and not necessarily against the Russian Empire, which may not have been supremely popular but did offer some prospects for Baltic advancement and autonomy. Krišjānis Valdemārs, a prominent Young Latvian, supported the extension of Russian administrative models in the hope that they would give greater scope to the replacement of traditional

German administrators by educated and aspirant Latvians. In 1905 Jaan Tönisson wrote that 'Estonia and Latvia are living borders of Russia against the West': the pattern of Baltic history meant that it was still the Germans, not the Russians, who were seen as the greater potential threat.[6]

The nationalist movement diversified from the 1880s, when a second generation of nationalists began to challenge the primacy of existing institutions. In Latvia this 'New Current' saw the existing movement, including vehicles of nationalist activism like the Young Latvians and the Riga Latvian Association, as broadly representative of Latvian merchants and property owners. The New Current sought to transcend these older bodies and to speak for the whole of the Latvian nation, including the working class and landless peasantry.[7] In Estonia the later movement was split between those who wished to cooperate with Baltic German liberal elements, and those who wanted to use the structures of the Russian Empire to promote Estonian autonomy. The second grouping, known as the 'Saint Petersburg Patriots', wanted the extension of Russian administrative reforms, like the *zemstva* (regional governing bodies equivalent to county councils) to the Baltic provinces to break the power of the Baltic German landowners. In 1881 Carl Robert Jakobson, a nationalist writer, politician and newspaper editor, led an Estonian delegation to St Petersburg to ask for the reorganisation of all ethnic Estonians into one administrative unit within the Russian Empire. These competing positions were represented in the early 20th century by two of the leaders of the national movement, Jaan Tönisson and Konstantin Päts. Tönisson was editor of *Postimees* from 1896, and continued to advocate co-operation with liberal elements amongst the Baltic Germans. He saw the Baltic as a historically distinctive world. Although he felt that conflict with the Russian central government was point-less, he believed that Estonians should be concerned with their own affairs, and not with all-Russian problems.[8] Päts edited *Teataja* (The Herald), based in Tallinn, from 1901 to 1905. He took Jakobson's line on the extension of Russian institutions into the Baltic provinces in order to create more opportunity for Estonians.

Lithuania's history of independent statehood and empire meant that, when national consciousness began to develop in the late 19th century, progress towards the idea of an independent state (rather than emphasis on cultural identity or political autonomy) was rapid. One of the first to put forward this idea was Jonas Basanavičius, editor of the first Lithuanian language newspaper, *Aušra* (The Dawn), which began publication in 1883. Although it had no specific political programme, it called for greater use of and respect for the Lithuanian language, and for an independent Lithuanian state, on the model of newly independent Bulgaria, in which Basanavičius had spent some time. Other national newspapers developed in the wake of *Aušra* – *Varpas* (The Bell), and *Tevynes Sargas* (The Guardian of the Homeland).[9] Lithuanian nationalists abroad tended to be even more strident – a Lithuanian-language newspaper was actually published in America several years before publication of *Aušra* began.

The Lithuanian national movement also had a complicated relationship with Polish nationalism. Seeing themselves as the larger partner in the ancient Polish-Lithuanian alliance, some Poles wanted to co-ordinate Lithuanian activities. Others dismissed the national movement completely, as being either a Russian or German attempt to drive a wedge between Poles and Lithuanians. The fact that Lithuanians might choose Russian language or culture over Polish seemed to some an unacceptable betrayal of an older historic partnership.[10] Attempts to encourage this tendency on the part of the Russian government intensified after Lithuanian involvement in the 1863 Polish uprising. The Imperial Government saw the Lithuanians as the less militant, more easily Russified junior partner, and tried to win the support of the Lithuanian peasantry by offering them special privileges at the expense of the Polish nobility. In this way they sought to obviate the 'Polish question' in this part of the Empire. The Governor-General of Vilnius, Nikolai Muraviev, claimed he could make the provinces of Kaunas and Vilnius completely Russian within 40 years. Lithuanian peasants were given generous opportunities to buy land from the Polish nobility after the emancipation of the 1860s; educational opportunities within Russia were made available to young Lithuanians such as Basanavičius and later Voldemaras. Lithuanian hostility to the historical Polonisation of Lithuanian culture was easily exploited. In fact by the turn of the century the antagonism between Poles and Lithuanians in Lithuanian territory was so severe that the Russian government backed away from this strategy as it posed a threat to good order.[11]

Unfortunately Russification proved to be equally unpopular, and cultural Russification policies backfired spectacularly. Legislation enforcing publication in Cyrillic rather than Latin script caused a violent reaction amongst Lithuanians, on national and cultural but also religious grounds. Use of Latin script distinguished the Roman Catholic from the Orthodox Church, and as such the imposition of Cyrillic was interpreted as an attempt to convert the Lithuanian population to Orthodoxy. A significant opponent of Russification in Lithuania was Bishop Motiejus Valančius. The author of religious and secular works aimed at the Lithuanian peasantry himself, he encouraged his clergy to write and teach in Lithuanian. Lithuania-language books were published abroad, in Germany and in the USA, and Valančius organised the smuggling of these works into the country, which continued over a period of four decades. The works in question focused on Lithuanian language, history and folklore, and were intended to raise the national consciousness of their readers. One of these publications was Basanavičius's *Aušra*. The Tsarist government eventually had to lift their ban on Lithuanian-language works in Latin script in 1904.[12]As Russian administrators of the time were well aware, the measure had backfired not simply because it encouraged anti-Russian feeling amongst Lithuanians, but also because it gave control of what the Lithuanian public was reading to illegal book smugglers rather than the local Russian authorities.[13] By this time the Catholic clergy was losing influence to younger, more secular publicists, who often celebrated Lithuania's pagan past and focused strongly on the idea of a return to an independent Lithuanian state.

A key issue for the Lithuanian nationalist movement at the turn of the century was the 'Lithuanianisation' of Vilnius. As nationalists looked back to the Grand Duchy of Lithuania for their inspiration for a new, though admittedly smaller, Lithuanian state, their national capital seemed to them important: it had to be reclaimed, notwithstanding its long history as an international and multicultural city. A group of Lithuanian intellectuals in Vilnius known as the 'Twelve Apostles' worked to restore Lithuanian culture in the city, with considerable success. They restored Mass in Lithuanian at St Michael's Church and a Lithuanian publishing house, printing press, bookshop, school and newspaper (*Vilniaus Žinios* – Vilnius News) were founded in the early years of the 20th century.[14] The idea of restoring a Lithuanian state was widely discussed, although more vocally abroad than at home – for example in American Lithuanian newspapers and in lectures in the European capitals.

By the latter years of the 19th century industrialisation was rapidly underway in Estonia and Livonia. This led to a significant movement of population into the towns and cities. By the turn of the century, Riga was the sixth largest city in the Russian Empire. This movement led to the creation not only of a native proletariat, but also of a new native middle class. By the beginning of the 20th century the proportion of Estonians and Latvians occupying positions in regional administration (for example on town councils) was rising.

In Lithuania relatively slow industrial development, in combination with political repression, led to large-scale emigration overseas, particularly to the United States of America. The tens of thousands of Lithuanian émigrés in the United States also played an important part in the national movement, as they had an active national cultural life: a Lithuanian-language newspaper, *Gazieta Lietuviszka*, began publication in 1879. There were Lithuanian orchestras, theatre groups and choirs in the USA. The Lithuanians even had an exhibit at the World Exhibition in Paris in 1900, in which they drew attention to Tsarist restrictions on Lithuanian culture.

In addition to liberal nationalist political involvement, social democratic parties were founded across the Baltic region – in Lithuania in 1896, Latvia in 1904 and Estonia in 1905. There were waves of strike action in the early years of the century, and when revolution broke out in St Petersburg in January 1905 disturbances quickly spread to the Baltic provinces. There were strikes and riots in all the major cities, as well as in the countryside, where manor houses were burned and Baltic German landowners attacked.

The crisis in St Petersburg dragged on through the year, culminating in a general strike which brought communications and industry across the Russian Empire to a halt in October 1905. Tsar Nicholas II was obliged to grant the October Manifesto, which made provision for a representative assembly with legislative powers, freedom of speech and assembly. Against this background all the Baltic national movements shifted away from their longstanding cultural concerns and became more politicised. In November 1905 800 representatives of different political groups met in the first pan-Estonian assembly, to discuss the issues of national unification and autonomy. Around 300 moderates led by Tönisson found themselves outnumbered by 500 assorted radicals and social democrats. Each wing issued a declaration demanding autonomy for Estonia, but the radicals tended to favour revolutionary rather than evolutionary tactics, and to unite Estonian questions with the wider Russian situation.[15]

In Latvia a series of congresses were held in November. A Teachers' Congress and a Rural Delegates' Congress both passed resolutions relating to local control of educational and rural affairs, and demanded a constituent assembly for Russia.[16] The idea of a federal structure for the Russian Empire, to include an autonomous Latvia, began to gain currency.

In November 1905 a committee of leading Lithuanian nationalists, headed by Basanavičius, convened Lithuania's first national assembly, the Grand Vilnius Seimas, or Grand Diet of Vilnius. Around 2,000 delegates – elected locally or simply looking to take part in the proceedings – arrived in Vilnius. The delegates made calls for Lithuanian autonomy within ethnic Lithuanian boundaries – something along the lines of the Grand Duchy of Finland – and for a democratically-elected parliament in Vilnius. Relations with other states within Russia were to be established upon a federative basis.

These November congresses proved to be the high-water mark of the nationalist surge. The Tsar's October Manifesto divided the revolutionary movement in the Baltic provinces as elsewhere. More liberal elements, including the Young Latvians, saw the opportunities that the Manifesto offered for constitutional government and involvement in political affairs as real progress. Socialists saw it as an attempt to split the movement by placating the middle classes – if the revolution continued the Tsarist monarchy might fall. The revolution was crushed militarily in the Baltic by Tsarist troops and Baltic German militias, who put down the uprising in the countryside.

The October Manifesto did usher in a period of relative freedom between 1905 and 1907 in which political groups and parties could operate. A representative assembly, the Duma, was established, in which the new political parties would be represented. Newspapers proliferated. Ants Piip edited a newspaper called *Hääl* (The Voice), in Kuressaare in 1906–7. He also founded the local Estonian Association on Saaremaa, and was its president between 1908 and 1912. A 'Young Estonia' movement was founded in 1906, essentially a cultural movement which encouraged its followers to 'remain Estonians but become Europeans'. Representatives of the Baltic nationalities participated in the First and Second Dumas, including Tönisson and Päts for Estonia, Jānis Goldmanis and Jānis Čakste (who was involved with the Russian Constitutional Democrats in the signing of the Vyborg Manifesto) for Latvia. The Lithuanians formed voting blocs with urban Jewish workers, which allowed them to send a number of representatives to the earlier Dumas.[17] Martynas Yčas, who would later accompany Voldemaras to the Paris Peace Conference, was a high-ranking Kadet in the fourth Duma, and served as Vice Minister of Education in the first Provisional Government of 1917. Electoral reforms introduced by the Russian Prime Minister Petr Stolypin in 1907 brought an end to this period of relative freedom and wide participation in the Duma, and drastically reduced representation by Russia's minority national groups, giving 200,000 Russians the electoral weight of 2.5 million Lithuanians.

Nevertheless the Duma period gave Baltic nationalists the opportunity for political involvement and experience. Further proposals for autonomy emerged in the period leading up to 1914, such as the scheme submitted by a Latvian Menshevik in 1912 (never acted upon) for the administrative unification of the ethnically Latvian areas of Kurzeme and Vidzeme. Important contributions to the burgeoning literature on the national question included M Skujenieks' *The National Question in Latvia* (1913), and M Valters' *The Question of Our Nationality, Ideas on the Present and Future of Latvia* (1914).[18] At the outbreak of war, thriving national movements existed in all three Baltic provinces, in which Piip, Meierovics and Voldemaras, in their late twenties and early thirties at this time, were playing a growing role.

3
War, Revolution and Independence

Russia's entry into the war against the Central Powers prompted displays of patriotic enthusiasm from ethnic Russians and subject nationalities alike. There was a general hope amongst Russian liberals that co-operation with the war effort would lead to a greater involvement on the part of civil society in the government of the Empire. Amongst national minorities this took the form of a hope for a greater degree of control over their own affairs as a quid pro quo for loyal support for the Russian war effort. On 8 August members of the state Duma reaffirmed their loyalty to the Russian Empire. Among those who took this oath were Jānis Goldmanis, who represented both Estonians and Latvians, and Martynas Yčas, who spoke for the Lithuanian population. Yčas asked that any peace settlement at the end of the War should secure the annexation of parts of East Prussia that contained significant Lithuanian populations – not to absorb them but to make them part of a Lithuanian state within a Russian federation. The Russian Prime Minister Ivan Goremykin reportedly dismissed Yčas's request as 'nonsense'.[1] Few can have been blind to the prospect, vocalised by the Latvian socialist

Miķelis Valters, that co-operation with Germany might help secure Baltic independence in some form, but this attracted little support on the outbreak of War. Even representatives of the Baltic German population pledged their continued allegiance to the Russian Imperial Family.[2]

The Russian military, attempting to meet French demands for an early offensive on Germany's eastern front while preventing their Polish salient from being cut off, launched simultaneous offensives in East Prussia and in Galicia. Serious defeats were inflicted on the Austro-Hungarian armies, and Galicia was largely overrun. But in the East Prussian campaign, against better trained and officered German units, the Russian drive came to grief at the Battles of Tannenberg and Masurian Lakes. Losses in both campaigns were huge. From the spring of 1915 onwards the German army took back all the territory the Central Powers had lost, pushed the Russians out of Poland, and moved into Lithuania and Courland. Kaunas was under siege by August 1915, and on 19 September 1915 the German army entered Vilnius. During the German advance peasants were ordered to burn their villages and relocate, on foot, into the interior of the Russian empire. Those who were regarded as politically unreliable (particularly Jews) were moved away from the front into the Russian interior.

By mid-1915 the front line had halted just short of Riga. It was in this context that a group of liberals and students led by the Duma deputy Jānis Goldmanis approached the Russian government and asked permission to organise a unit of Latvian volunteers for the defence of Latvian territory. As a general principle this kind of national territorial army would have been frowned upon by the government, and earlier in the War this request would almost certainly have been denied, but the critical situation in the Baltic in mid-1915 meant that the request could hardly be refused. Zigfrīds Meierovics worked on the organising committee of the Latvian rifle units, which grew from battalions into regiments as Latvians transferred there from other units and new conscripts were also assigned to them – the regiments came to total as many as 30–40,000 men. They were renowned for their military successes in the defence of Riga (not taken by the German army until August 1917), and besides being a vital component of the Imperial Russian Army they played an important role in increasing Latvian national consciousness during the War.[3] Typically for a middle-class liberal Baltic nationalist, Meierovics worked with a number of civil society organisations involved in the war effort – at the outbreak of War the All-Russian Municipal Union, for whom he organised food supplies for the northern front from a base in Rēzekne in Latgale, and from 1915 the Latvian Refugee Association which operated across the Empire, giving assistance to those who had been forcibly relocated from the Latvian provinces.[4] Ants Piip, working for the Russian government in St Petersburg, would also have been deeply involved in the war effort. Augustinas Voldemaras took up a position at the University of Perm during the war years.

The first German incursions into the Baltic provinces awakened interest in the German military and Foreign Office in the possibility of detaching these areas from the Russian Empire. General Erich Ludendorff wrote of his first exposure to the Baltic region that 'because of a lack of publications in German we knew very little of the land and its people; we felt as if in a new world'.[5] From November 1915 the occupied Lithuanian and Latvian territories, known as the *Land Oberost*, were effectively governed by the German High Command, which requisitioned goods but also carried out a policy of 'Germanisation'.

The existence of the Baltic German nobility in Estonia and Latvia seemed to offer an ideal opportunity for the creation of satellite states under German control. Despite the lack of a German elite class in Lithuania, Lithuanian separatists were nevertheless encouraged to think in terms of an independent Lithuania closely allied with, and protected by, Germany. These schemes initially faced some opposition from the German Chancellor Theobald von Bethmann-Hollweg, as they seemed to jeopardise any chance of a separate peace with Russia – which was vital if the Germans were to be able to turn their full strength against the Allies in the west. By the middle of 1916, however, the German government had accepted that some form of union of the Baltic provinces with the German Reich was both desirable and possible. Such schemes already extended to Estonia and Livonia, which had not yet been conquered. Towards the end of the War, when the ideal of national self-determination increasingly gained currency, the language in which these schemes were presented was tempered so as to focus on independence within a German orbit rather than complete union with the German Reich.

Renewed demands for autonomy (in the case of Estonia and Latvia) and independence (in the case of Lithuania) therefore developed in three different contexts: within the increasingly discontented and revolutionary Russian empire; in the Baltic territories occupied by the German army; and amongst Baltic nationalists abroad. During the War Lithuanian information bureaux were set up in France, Switzerland and Scandinavia, often with American-Lithuanian backing. Conferences were held at which emigrants and political refugees demanded complete Lithuanian independence. The American Relief Fund for Lithuanian War Sufferers, set up by the Reverend A Milukas, lobbied President Woodrow Wilson for support, with the result that the President declared 1 November 1916 'Lithuanian Day'. Over $200,000 was raised by local war-relief committees on that day.[6] Latvian social democrats like Miķelis Valters and Felikss Cielēns were also active internationally in promoting plans for Latvian autonomy.[7]

Within Russia, the outbreak of revolution in Petrograd in February 1917 changed the political landscape completely. Although prompted by food shortages, industrial unrest and Russia's continually poor performance in the War, the initial revolutionary outbreak took many by surprise. In the wake of the Tsar's abdication, two centres of power emerged – the liberal Provisional Government, composed of members of the Duma, and the workers and soldiers councils, or soviets, which were established on the model of 1905. This duality of power was replicated in the Baltic region. Liberal middle-class parties were founded, such as the Latvian Farmers Union, led by Kārlis Ulmanis. Meierovics attended its first congress at around this time. However, there was also active co-operation between socialists in the Baltic provinces and the socialist leadership, whether Socialist Revolutionary, Menshevik or Bolshevik, in the Petrograd Soviet.

Kārlis Ulmanis (1877–1942) was a professional agriculturalist and sometime academic who studied in Switzerland and Germany. He became a prominent Latvian politician. Imprisoned following the 1905 revolution, he was in exile in the USA until 1913. He was the founder of the Latvian Farmers' Union and a key figure in the proclamation of independence in November 1918. He served as Latvia's first Prime Minister, and in several subsequent governments. He staged a coup in May 1934 and installed an authoritarian regime, taking over the presidency in 1936. Following the Soviet occupation he was dismissed and deported. He died of dysentery in Krasnovodsk in 1942.

The main demand of the liberal Baltic middle classes in the spring of 1917 was for the reorganisation of their territories into single administrative units along ethnic lines. Estonian leaders began discussions with the Provisional Government on this issue almost immediately after the February Revolution. Much of this discussion was couched in terms of local self-government: the Estonian Duma deputies Jaan Tönisson and Jaan Raamot agreed that their best tactic was to make initial demands which would be broadly acceptable to the Provisional Government. On 26 March 40,000 people attended a demonstration in Petrograd in support of this measure. The Provisional Government issued a law four days later (30 March) which unified Estonian territories into one administrative unit. An elected assembly, the Maapäev, was set up. However, the law did not make clear exactly what responsibilities were to be devolved to the Maapäev, and this would be a source of antagonism between the Provisional Government and the Maapäev throughout 1917.[8]

Latvian demands for similar consideration were less successful. Some ethnic Latvian territory was occupied by the German army, and ethnically Latvian Latgale formed part of the Russian province of Vitebsk. In the spring of 1917 Latvian liberal demands were as follows: Russia to be a federative republic, autonomy for Latvia, the incorporation of Latgale in Latvia, and recognition of the principle of national, not just territorial, autonomies. Their programme was summed up in the Latvian revolutionary slogan 'A Free Latvia in a Free Russia', which was widely used before 1917 and became ubiquitous during the revolutionary year. Meierovics saw the unity of ethnic Latvians within one national entity as a basic prerequisite for the creation of a Latvian republic, which was now his ultimate goal – though this republic did not have to be a sovereign state.[9] The right of Latvians to national self-determination could best be achieved, in his opinion, through a federal solution. Latvian social democrats also supported these basic demands, but were more inclined, and earlier, towards greater autonomy or even independence.

Negotiations on this issue continued throughout 1917. Five leading Latvian liberal politicians were present at a conference with President Alexander Kerensky at the Winter Palace on 19 September 1917 – Zigfrīds Meierovics, Adolfs Klīve, Voldemars Zāmuels, Jānis Goldmanis and Jānis Zalatis. Otto Karklins, a Latvian Bolshevik, was also there. According to Klīve's account of this meeting, Meierovics said that *Latvia should be granted autonomy without delay as a proof that the new order does not intend to reduce Latvia and the Latvians to a lower order than they were under tsarism and German baronage. That must be done immediately in order to tie Latvia to the great Russian revolution and the Empire with unbreakable bonds.* At that moment one of Kerensky's aides entered the room and announced that the 20 minutes allotted for the interview were over, and that the Prime Minister's next visitor was waiting. Kerensky replied to Meierovics that the Latvians most certainly would receive the right of self-determination, through the operation of a similar system to the *zemstva* in Russia, but that political autonomy was unthinkable, because in that case similar rights would have to be

> 'Latvia should be granted autonomy without delay as a proof that the new order does not intend to reduce Latvia and the Latvians to a lower order than they were under tsarism and German baronage. That must be done immediately in order to tie Latvia to the great Russian revolution and the Empire with unbreakable bonds.'
>
> MEIEROVICS IN AN INTERVIEW WITH KERENSKY IN SEPTEMBER 1917

granted to all nationalities living in Russia, and that would be impossible.[10]

In Lithuania, the German occupation meant that there were two forums for discussion of independence: one in German-occupied Vilnius, and one in Petrograd. A Lithuanian National Council was formed in March 1917, which convened a Lithuanian congress in Petrograd in June. There was a division between right-wing deputies who wanted complete independence, and those further to the left who wanted a free Lithuania in a Russian federation, on the Latvian model. Later in 1917 a conference was allowed to be held under German supervision to discuss the future of the Lithuanian state. Elections could not be held, so leading Lithuanians drew up a list of well-known people in each district and invited them. This was the Vilnius Conference held between 18–22 September 1917 and attended by 222 delegates. The conference elected a 20-member council, the Taryba, to act as the Lithuanian peoples' authority. Antanas Smetona was the chairman.

Antanas Smetona (1874–1944) was a Lithuanian lawyer and journalist, involved in national student activism from the 1890s, then in politics and publishing. He was active in pro-German politics in Vilnius during the occupation, and chairman of the Taryba when it declared independence in February 1918. He fled Lithuania at the end of 1918, but was named President on his return in April 1919. He was out of power between 1920 and 1926, when he was installed as an authoritarian president after a nationalist coup. Amidst internal divisions over whether and how to resist the Soviet occupation in June 1940 he fled to Germany and ultimately to the USA, where he died in a fire in 1944.

In late 1917, the Taryba engaged in negotiations with the German government about the terms of a declaration of independence which would make clear Lithuania's dependence on Germany. The Germans were keen to have this as part of their forthcoming peace negotiations with the Soviet government.

The first draft, agreed in December 1917, declared the restoration of Lithuania as an independent state, with Vilnius as its capital, but declared the Taryba to be 'in favour of the Lithuanian state's firm and perpetual bond of alliance with Germany'. There was no mention of a constituent assembly, and the Germans refused to permit this. This caused radical members of the Taryba to walk out. To convince the left wing Taryba members to return Smetona resigned, and the veteran Lithuanian nationalist Jonas Basanavičius succeeded him as chairman. On 16 February a new resolution was approved in which the Taryba, as 'the sole representative of the Lithuanian nation' declared 'the restoration of an independent, democratically organized Lithuanian state', along with 'the abolition of all political ties which have existed with other nations'.[11] It was on the basis of the December Declaration that the German government accorded recognition of Lithuania's independence in March 1918, but the February Declaration was always later used to mark the emergence of the independent state of Lithuania. February 16th became independence day in the new Lithuanian state.

The Baltic nationalities were not alone in the Russian Empire in voicing demands for autonomy, or independence, in the wake of the February Revolution. In September 1917 the Ukrainian governing body, the Rada, invited representatives of all non-Russian nationalities within the empire to the Congress of Non-Sovereign Nations (sometimes called the Nationalities Congress, or Congress of Small Nations) in Kiev. The Congress took place between 8 and 11 September. Ants Piip, Zigfrīds Meierovics and Augustinas Voldemaras were all in attendance. This may have been the first time that Piip and Meierovics met, and as the Estonians and Latvians co-operated closely at the Congress they developed a good working relationship.[12] This sort of co-operation between the border states would continue after independence and at the Paris Peace Conference. The Baltic representatives admired the Ukrainian Rada for taking the lead in its defiant stance towards the Provisional Government. The Ukrainians were also important allies because, in contrast to the Baltic nationalities, 'there were 40 million of them'. Meierovics, who was one of ten Latvian delegates at the Congress, made a speech in which he demonstrated this appreciation of the Ukrainian move, outlined Latvia's demands, but also made it clear that their demands did not threaten Russia's unity or welfare:

The Central Ukrainian Rada, whose guests we are, is in the avant-garde of our [Russia's] nationalities. She was the first to raise her voice and demand her rights. She was the first one to have thought about the fate of other nations and summoned us here. The Central Ukrainian Rada, the oldest of our sisters, deserves heartfelt gratitude from devastated Latvia and a warm handshake from the Latvian people. (Applause) *At the moment when our hands slackened, and we did not see any help for our people, in the moment when Latvia is threatened to be crushed between two millstones, the call of the Ukrainians arrived: 'Come and we shall close the ranks, we shall struggle together for our rights, for the struggle has only begun!' We shall fight until victory for the welfare of our people. But to gain victory we Russia's non-sovereign peoples must become allies in the true meaning of the word. We must form one unified front, against all who are opposed to the principle of self-determination.* (Applause) *Here in beautiful Kiev, the cradle of people's autonomy, we shall leave behind us the headquarters for our unified struggle – the Council of Peoples. To this organ, properly constituted, we shall entrust the convening of – even before Russia's*

Constituent Assembly meets – the Constituent Assembly of Nations, which then will judiciously determine the future of Russia's nationalities. (Applause) ... *We recognize that these our moderate demands do not threaten the unity of Russia's state and do not impair its general welfare. Therefore we are imploring the Provisional Government at this moment of Russia's history to issue and announce a special decree, recognizing the above demands. However, – the Latvians shall struggle for their political demands until victory or defeat* (Prolonged applause).[13]

Augustinas Voldemaras also spoke at the conference, but rather than calling for autonomy he spoke in favour of complete independence for Lithuania. He was particularly disillusioned by the attitude of liberal Russians to the demands of the Nationalities Congress, and he saw this as a turning point in the attitude of the small nations in the debate on federation or independence. He later described his experience at the Congress in an interview with James Simpson of the British Foreign Office. *My experience, particularly after the Kiev Congress in September 1917, is that none of the small peoples believe in the possibility of a Federation under Great Russia. Thus Kerensky sent down Slavinski to that Congress of representatives of all the nationalities in the Russian Empire other than Great Russia, to exercise control over what was said. One result was that the Press was not allowed to print my speeches urging complete independence. The Great Russian intention is to reconstruct the Russian State exactly as it was previous to August 1914, with the exception of Poland. My impression however, is that anarchy will persist in Russia for another couple of decades.*[14]

The nationalities question was not the only issue that the Provisional Government failed to address during 1917. Largely as a result of its provisional nature (its members saw it as a body designed only to govern until elections to an all-Russian constituent assembly could be held) it failed to deal decisively with the land question, and perhaps more importantly it continued the hugely unpopular war. As a result the influence of the one party that had distanced itself from the Provisional Government completely, the Bolsheviks, grew steadily in the autumn of 1917. The growth of Bolshevik influence in Russia was matched and in some cases outpaced by similar growth in the Baltic provinces. In Estonia well-organised Bolshevik groups in Tallinn and Narva made significant gains in local elections in September 1917. The Central Committee of the Latvian Social Democratic Party had been under Bolshevik control since 1914, and the party won 60 per cent of the votes in elections to a Livonian provincial assembly in September. There was no real opposition to Bolshevik control in the Baltic provinces after the October Revolution, and popular support for the regional Bolshevik parties was confirmed in the results of the election to the all-Russian constituent assembly in November 1917. On 28 November the Estonian Maapäev was disbanded by the Bolshevik Military Revolutionary Committee.

The October Revolution had the effect of reversing liberal and radical opinion on the issue of independence. While the socialist emphasis now was on internationalism and close links with the Soviet state, the bourgeois liberal parties had little choice but to oppose a Russian government which they did not recognise. Ants Piip articulated the Estonian position after the overthrow of the Provisional Government as follows: *We took the attitude that, on the overthrow of the Provisional Government, all legal authority everywhere in Russia ceased to exist. The Russian State, as such, was dissipated, and only the various parts that remained in different hands resulted. There was not only a 'vacancy of power', but also a 'vacancy of sovereignty'; the old Russian state simply ceased to exist ... With the overthrow of Kerensky the territory of the Empire became a* res nullius, *belonging to nobody in general, but capable of individual appropriation by different nationalities. Nobody owned Russia; it was left to every group to help itself. Therefore we dealt, by a sort of implicit recognition, with other groups who had been, along with us, within the former Russian Empire, and treated them as co-successors. It was not even a* de facto *relationship; it was the realization that we had all come out of the same pot.*[15]

A Committee of Elders – Konstantin Päts, Konstantin Konik and Jüri Vilms – had been nominated by the Maapäev before its dissolution, and this committee declared the country's independence on 24 February, as German forces approached Tallinn. There was no time for Latvians in Latvia to take similar action, but a Latvian National Council was established in Petrograd – Zigfrīds Meierovics joined its foreign relations department. The brief period of Bolshevik rule in the Baltic was brought to an end by the German occupation of the entire region. In March 1918 the Soviet Government signed the Treaty of Brest-Litovsk, in which they abandoned Courland, Riga and the Estonian island of Saaremaa. A supplementary agreement in August gave up Estonia and Livonia as well, though these too had been under German control since February 1918. During the course of the negotiations the Bolshevik delegation produced Latvian and Lithuanian Bolsheviks (Pēteris Stučka for Latvia and Vincas Kapsukas for Lithuania), who testified to the revolutionary nature of the Baltic populations. However, there was also a second Lithuanian delegate present at the conference – Augustinas

Voldemaras, who had made his way to the Ukraine and convinced the Ukrainian delegation to accept him as 'Lithuanian advisor' to their delegation.[16]

During the German occupation, political institutions continued to be controlled or suppressed. The Maapäev, disbanded by the Bolsheviks in November, was not permitted to reconvene. In Lithuania the Taryba briefly elected a Catholic member of the German princely house of Württemberg as 'Mindaugas II', King of Lithuania, in July 1918. Voldemaras, who returned to Lithuania from Russia in mid-1918 and was co-opted to the Taryba, disapproved. The Baltic German population of the Baltic provinces had been completely alienated by the Bolshevik revolution, and the German occupation gave them the opportunity to press for annexation to the German Empire. The scene was set for the German occupation to crystallise into a longer-term colonisation of the eastern Baltic, but for this to happen Germany had to win the War in the west. The defeat of Germany in November 1918 created a vacuum of power that allowed Baltic national governments to take control. The Maapäev was reformed. A Bolshevik Russian invasion of Estonia in November 1918 was repulsed by native Estonian forces under Johan Laidoner, a former Tsarist officer, with the help of

Konstantin Päts (1874–1956) was a Tallinn lawyer of peasant background. In 1901 he founded the socialist Estonian-language newspaper *Teataja*. Exiled after the 1905 Revolution and imprisoned briefly on his return, he was a key figure in the national movement. Active in war relief work, he was a member of the Committee of Elders that proclaimed Estonian independence, and he led the first provisional government. He led seven Estonian governments between 1918 and 1934. In 1933–4 he took power and closed parliament and political parties, becoming President in 1938. He was removed from power and deported in July 1940. He died in a Soviet psychiatric hospital in Tver in 1956.

Finnish volunteers and the British navy. Independence was proclaimed in Latvia on 18 November, and a government headed by Kārlis Ulmanis, the leader of the Farmers' Union, began the struggle against a Soviet invasion. Zigfrīds Meierovics became Latvian Foreign Minister.

Two factors, then, made the emergence of national governments in Estonia, Latvia and Lithuania possible. Firstly, the Bolshevik Revolution removed the authority that liberal politicians had recognised. Secondly, the German defeat in the World War created a vacuum which gave the liberal national governments the opportunity to take power. But a third factor was crucial as a new source of optimism and a focus for cultivating support: the Western Allies and their articulation of support for national self-determination.

Voldemaras visited Switzerland in the autumn of 1918 with Smetona and Yčas and returned with promises of support from representatives of the American Lithuanian population. The Taryba chose Voldemaras (over Jurgis Šaulys, a veteran nationalist and one of the signatories of the declaration of independence) as Prime Minister, and he was charged with organising a cabinet. In a speech to the Taryba on 14 November, he expressed his optimism about Lithuania's future as a small independent state in the new Europe. Lithuania would be a neutral state, and would not need a large army to protect herself – the doctrine of national self-determination would be enough. *The new world brings a new light. From the great American democracy comes joyous news – down with force, replace it with justice. It is clearly written in President Wilson's program: both large and small nations have the same rights.*[17]

The new governments of Estonia, Latvia and Lithuania faced an increasingly complex military and political situation

PRESIDENT WILSON'S FOURTEEN POINTS, 8 JANUARY 1918

The program of the world's peace, therefore, is our program; and that program, the only possible program, as we see it, is this:

I. Open covenants of peace, openly arrived at, after which there shall be no private international understandings of any kind but diplomacy shall proceed always frankly and in the public view.

II. Absolute freedom of navigation upon the seas, outside territorial waters, alike in peace and in war, except as the seas may be closed in whole or in part by international action for the enforcement of international covenants.

III. The removal, so far as possible, of all economic barriers and the establishment of an equality of trade conditions among all the nations consenting to the peace and associating themselves for its maintenance.

IV. Adequate guarantees given and taken that national armaments will be reduced to the lowest point consistent with domestic safety.

V. A free, open-minded, and absolutely impartial adjustment of all colonial claims, based upon a strict observance of the principle that in determining all such questions of sovereignty the interests of the populations concerned must have equal weight with the equitable claims of the government whose title is to be determined.

VI. The evacuation of all Russian territory and such a settlement of all questions affecting Russia as will secure the best and freest cooperation of the other nations of the world in obtaining for her an unhampered and unembarrassed opportunity for the independent determination of her own political development and national policy and assure her of a sincere welcome into the society of free nations under institutions of her own choosing; and, more than a welcome, assistance also of every kind that she may need and may herself desire. The treatment accorded Russia by her sister nations in the months to come will be the acid test of their good will, of their comprehension of her needs as distinguished from their own interests, and of their intelligent and unselfish sympathy.

VII. Belgium, the whole world will agree, must be evacuated and restored, without any attempt to limit the sovereignty which she enjoys in common with all other free nations. No other single act will serve as this will serve to restore confidence among the nations in the laws which they have themselves set and determined for the government of their relations with one another. Without this healing act the whole structure and validity of international law is forever impaired.

VIII. All French territory should be freed and the invaded portions restored, and the wrong done to France by Prussia in 1871 in the matter of Alsace-Lorraine, which has unsettled the peace of the world for nearly fifty years, should be righted, in order that peace may once more be made secure in the interest of all.

IX. A readjustment of the frontiers of Italy should be effected along clearly recognizable lines of nationality.

X. The peoples of Austria-Hungary, whose place among the nations we wish to see safeguarded and assured, should be accorded the freest opportunity to autonomous development.

XI. Rumania, Serbia, and Montenegro should be evacuated; occupied territories restored; Serbia accorded free and secure access to the sea; and the relations of the several Balkan states to one another determined by friendly counsel along historically established lines of allegiance and nationality; and international guarantees of the political and economic independence and territorial integrity of the several Balkan states should be entered into.

XII. The Turkish portion of the present Ottoman Empire should be assured a secure sovereignty, but the other nationalities which are now under Turkish rule should be assured an undoubted security of life and an absolutely unmolested opportunity of autonomous development, and the Dardanelles should be permanently opened as a free passage to the ships and commerce of all nations under international guarantees.

XIII. An independent Polish state should be erected which should include the territories inhabited by indisputably Polish populations, which should be assured a free and secure access to the sea, and whose political and economic independence and territorial integrity should be guaranteed by international covenant.

XIV. A general association of nations must be formed under specific covenants for the purpose of affording mutual guarantees of political independence and territorial integrity to great and small states alike.

during the course of 1919, and their success in fighting off Soviet invasion, German intrigues and Bolshevik sympathy amongst their own populations was by no means guaranteed. While for Voldemaras complete independence was what he had always sought, for Piip and Meierovics it was an unexpected consequence of the turmoil in Russia. Independence in this case was a consequence of political circumstances, rather than stemming from 'the plans or intentions of the dominant political movement'.[18]

Zigfrids Meierovics (1887–1925).

II
The Peace Conferences

4
Early Allied Contacts

The new Baltic governments had begun to make contacts with the representatives of the larger European powers during the course of 1918, with a view to securing recognition of their independence. As it began to seem increasingly likely that the Allies would win the War, building relationships with the Allied governments became a clear priority. In order to get a hearing at the forthcoming Peace Conference, it seemed, it would be vital to have Allied connections. This was true for all Russia's border states. Zourab Avalishvili, a prominent Georgian who arrived in London at the end of 1918, described his role as that of the 'switchman' – he would transfer his country's allegiance smoothly from Germany to the Allies.[1]

The first Estonian and Latvian contacts with Allied representatives took place in Petrograd in January 1918. Representatives of both states were in Petrograd for the meeting of the All-Russian Constituent Assembly, which was closed by the Bolsheviks after only one session. Estonian members of the assembly visited the British Chargé d'Affaires, Francis Lindley, the French Ambassador, M. Noulens, and the Counsellor of the American Embassy, Mr J Butler Wright. Ants Piip was present at the meeting at the American Embassy, along with Julius Seljamaa, a member of the Maapäev, but not, it seems, at the meeting at the British Embassy, where Jaan Poska, Commissioner for Estonia, and Jüri Vilms, another Maapäev Deputy and later a member of the Committee of Elders which would declare independence, accompanied Seljamaa. The case made in all three meetings was broadly the same. The Estonian representatives explained that their initial hope had been for an autonomous Estonia within a Russian federal republic, but that in the current circumstances this was of course impossible. The German government had offered them independence under a German protectorate, and if they refused this the Germans were likely to occupy the country. They were willing to resist the German occupation if they received assurances from the British, French and American governments that they would support Estonia's independence at the forthcoming Peace Conference.[2] All three Western diplomats gave sympathetic but non-committal responses. Lindley, with the approval of the British Foreign Secretary Arthur Balfour, issued a reply stating that the British government would do all it could at the Peace Conference to prevent the annexation of any state by Germany against its will, and to secure 'some form of international guarantee' of the independence of states that came into existence as a result

Jaan Poska (1866–1920) was an Estonian barrister and first Estonian mayor of Tallinn in 1904. He was again mayor of Tallinn in 1913–17. When the Provisional Government unified the administration of Estonia in April 1917 they named Poska Commissioner for Estonia. He established Estonian as the official language and organised elections to the Maapäev. On independence in 1918 Poska became Foreign Minister and during the German occupation worked in Western Europe for diplomatic recognition. He died in Tallinn in 1920.

of the War.[3] A delegation of Latvian representatives toured the three embassies at around the same time. Meierovics was present, with Jānis Seskis (later a member of the Latvian delegation in Paris), at all three meetings. They received similarly non-committal replies.

On 1 February 1918 a delegation of Estonian representatives, including Piip, Jaan Tönisson and Kaarel Pusta, made their way via Finland to Stockholm, to establish relations with both the Scandinavian governments and with Allied representatives in Scandinavia. Each delegate was equipped with 13,000 Kerensky roubles, a document accrediting them as a representative of the Estonian National Council, and a memorandum on Estonian independence which they had to translate into English and French. They eventually arrived in Stockholm, after an eventful journey, on 13 March.[4]

Stockholm in 1918 was, in the words of the British Ambassador to Sweden Sir Esme Howard, 'a meeting house for the leaders of various subject races who hoped to achieve independence after the collapse of the Romanov empire'.[5] None of the Scandinavian powers were willing to offer any sort of recognition, unless the Baltic governments could obtain statements of recognition from the German and Soviet governments. However, Tönisson made significant progress in a meeting with Howard in February. Howard was sympathetic to the idea of Baltic independence, and proved a useful contact, as he was later appointed as the British representative in charge of Northern Europe at the Peace Conference in Paris. Nevertheless, he was obliged to frame his response to the Estonian enquiry in the same terms as Francis Lindley had in Petrograd. The British Government would make sure the Estonians received favourable consideration at the Peace Conference, but if there were a possibility of Russia re-forming as a federal state then that would be preferable. Tönisson played on the imminent German invasion of Estonia, and emphasised that the elections to the Estonian Constituent Assembly showed a clear preference among the Estonian people for independence. He suggested that, if it were not possible for the British government to recognise Estonian independence outright, a possible solution might be for them to recognise the Estonian Constituent Assembly 'as a *de facto* independent body until the meeting of the Peace Conference'. The British Foreign Office readily agreed, and this discussion formed the basis for the *de facto* recognition extended to Estonia by both the British and French governments on 20 March 1918.[6]

Esme Howard (1863–1939) was a British diplomat and member of the leading British Catholic aristocratic family. He passed the diplomatic service exam in 1885 and served in Rome, Berlin, Crete, Washington and Vienna. He was Ambassador to Berne in 1911–13 and Stockholm in 1913–18, where he came into contact with various Baltic politicians. In 1919 he went with the British delegation to the Paris Peace Conference where he was in charge of Northern European affairs. He resumed his career as an ambassador in Madrid (1919–24) and Washington (1924–30). He retired with a peerage as Baron Howard of Penrith in 1930 and died in 1939.

Ants Piip and Kaarel Pusta, along with another Estonian representative Eduard Virgo, left Stockholm on 21 March for Oslo, where Virgo met the Norwegian Foreign Minister Nils Ihlen. They travelled to Bergen and boarded a mail ship to Britain, landing in Aberdeen and proceeding by train to London. They arrived in London on 9 April.[7] There was little awareness of events in Estonia in British Foreign Office circles. This ignorance about, and low regard for, the Baltic governments is nowhere better illustrated than in the tendentious and factually flawed account of the arrival of the Estonian delegation given by J D Gregory, the head of the Foreign Office's Northern Department. 'Virgo, Pusta and

Pup [*sic*] arrived in England and ... thereupon held a conference at which the subject of debate was the precise location of the centre of London. Virgo spoke first and said: "I know. It is Hammersmith Broadway": because once upon a time one of his compatriots had written to him from there to describe its great hubbub and congestion. Pusta then said: "No, Virgo, you are wrong. The centre of London is Bloomsbury": because he was a man of literary tastes. But Pup upped and said: "My dear friends, you are both wrong. The centre of London is the Savoy Hotel". And from this it will surprise no-one to learn that it was Pup who subsequently became Minister for Foreign Affairs under the style and title of Professor Piip; that being his real name – and the original pseudonym having been conveyed to us as such through a fault of decyphering.'[8]

However, there were some people with expertise. The Political Intelligence Department, which was charged with providing information on the many complex political and economic questions arising from the War in Europe, contained two specialists on Russian affairs, James Young Simpson and Rex Leeper. Simpson in particular proved to be an important contact, and would later work with Esme Howard in the British delegation at the Paris Peace Conference. The Estonian delegation managed to secure an interview with Balfour on 23 April, at which they submitted a memorandum which played up the anti-German sentiments of the Estonian people. The Foreign Secretary replied to them on 3 May in the following terms. 'It gave me much pleasure to receive your recent visit, and I take this opportunity of assuring you that His Majesty's Government greet with sympathy the aspirations of the Esthonian people and are glad to reaffirm their readiness to grant provisional recognition to the

Esthonian National Council as a *de facto* independent body until the Peace Conference takes place, when the future status of Esthonia ought to be settled as far as possible in accordance with the wishes of the population. It would obviously be impossible for His Majesty's Government at the present time to guarantee to Esthonia the right to participate at the conference, but at any such conference His Majesty's Government will do their utmost to ensure that the above principle is applied to Esthonia. In the meantime His Majesty's Government will be glad to receive Professor Antoine Piip as the informal representative of the Esthonian provisional government.'[9]

The delegation also submitted their memorandum to the American Embassy, but they received no reply. While other members of the delegation proceeded to Paris where they would receive similar assurances from M. Pichon, the French Minister for Foreign Affairs on 12 May, Piip remained in London for the time being as the official Estonian representative there. In the following months he made contact with the Japanese embassy in London, and with the unofficial Bolshevik representative in London, Maksim Litvinov – although relations with Litvinov were broken off after the Soviet invasion of Estonia in November 1918. He also took part in a meeting with Robert Cecil, Admiral Freemantle and Colonel Frederick Kisch, in which they made arrangements to assist the Estonian government through the supply of arms and through the presence of a naval squadron under Rear-Admiral Edwyn Alexander-Sinclair, and later under Admiral Walter Cowan, off the Baltic coast.[10]

No Latvian representative was sent abroad until August, when Zigfrīds Meierovics was dispatched to London. Jānis Čakste followed him shortly afterwards on a mission to

France. Meierovics had been specifically advised by the Latvian National Council to put himself in touch with the representatives of the other border states in London, and he quickly did so. This was the foundation of the policy of Baltic co-operation in which he was the driving force up until his death in 1925. He established good relations with Ants Piip, with Rudolf Holsti, the Finnish Foreign Minister, and David Ghambashidze, the Georgian representative in London. These men worked together to establish relationships with Foreign Office officials like Simpson and Leeper, and such other British experts on Baltic affairs as they could find. The Baltic diplomats met regularly at the Royal Society Club where they discussed the possibility of political and military co-operation between their countries. There were obvious benefits to such a policy for the Baltic governments and it was also to prove a useful tool in the campaign for Allied recognition, as it provided an answer to the often-asked question about how the Baltic states might preserve their independence in the face of a Russian or German threat. Holsti's interest in this kind of co-operation was prompted by sympathy for the other Baltic nationalities, but also by his own perception of the interests of Finnish foreign policy. He was attempting to distance Finland from its association with both Germany and Russia, and develop a new orientation for the country. As it was

Jānis Čakste (1859–28) was a Moscow-educated lawyer from Courland. He was already advocating Latvian autonomy when elected to the Duma in 1906. He was briefly imprisoned for organising protests against the Duma's dissolution. He was active in war relief work from 1915 and chair of the Central Committee for Latvian Refugees in 1917. He went to Stockholm to lobby for Latvian independence in 1918 and became chair of the National Council when it convened in November 1918 to proclaim Latvian independence. He was elected the first President of independent Latvia in 1922. He was re-elected in 1925 and died in office in 1927.

clear that the Allies regarded Finland as a German-oriented country, he was looking for a stance which would provide security but also appeal to them.[11]

Meierovics found life in London hard, as he had few personal contacts and accommodation cost so much that there was little money left for the job of promoting the Latvian cause.[12] Nevertheless he worked tirelessly to press the Latvian case on the British Government, submitting memoranda and canvassing individuals within the Foreign Office. On the day of the armistice, 11 November 1918, this hard work won him a declaration from Balfour along similar lines to that received by the Estonians back in May, although less definite in its tone. 'His Majesty's Government have viewed with the deepest sympathy the aspirations of the Lettish people and its desire for liberation from the German yoke. They are glad to reaffirm their readiness to grant provisional recognition to the Lettish National Council as a *de facto* independent body until such time as the Peace Conference lays the foundation of a new era of freedom and happiness for your people. In the meantime His Majesty's Government will be glad to receive you as the informal diplomatic representative of the Lettish Provisional Government.'[13]

The dispatch of Lithuanian representatives abroad was delayed until the autumn of 1918. This was in part a result of the political situation in Lithuania and the manner in which the Taryba had first been established – under a German protectorate. However, the Lithuanians benefited from the work of émigré organisations such as the Lithuanian National Council in Lausanne, and the Lithuanian Council in America. While there were Latvian and Estonian equivalents (the American Estonian League was one example), they were not as large or politically organised. Switzerland became the centre of Allied contacts with the Lithuanians in 1918. Dr Bartuška, the vice-president of the Lithuanian Council in America, made one of the first contacts with Allied representatives in February 1918, while on a visit to Switzerland. He distributed letters from the Taryba to the heads of state and foreign ministers of each of the Allied powers, explaining the history of the Lithuanian state and the extent of the territory the Taryba claimed to represent, and requesting recognition. Voldemaras himself visited Switzerland towards the end of October 1918, and toured the Allied embassies there. He informed the Allied diplomats that members of the Taryba were unanimously in favour of German withdrawal from the country, but they needed to know what support they might expect from the Allies. The Allied governments were less sympathetic to Lithuania than they were to either Estonia or Latvia, partly because the Taryba was considered to be a pro-German body. The American government was not willing to comment on Lithuania's future prior to the Peace Conference, and particularly not 'in view of the unsettled existing conditions'.[14]

The existence of a powerful Lithuanian émigré movement also created problems, however. In several instances it led to duplication of representation. For example, there were two Lithuanian press bureaux in Switzerland by the winter of 1918, one run by Juozas Gabrys, one of the most prominent Lithuanian nationalists in the West, and another established by Jurgis Šaulys, the representative of the Taryba. A subsequent acrimonious split between Gabrys and the Taryba proved particularly unfortunate given Gabrys's wealth of Western contacts. Two American Lithuanians, Jonas Šliupas and Tomas Naruševičius, arrived in London and set up a Lithuanian Information Bureau there in February 1918; they were shortly followed by two representatives of the Taryba,

Vladas Čepinskis and Kazimieras Bizauskas, who had been dispatched to London to establish formal representation there. In this case the two groups co-operated easily. In November 1918 the Taryba sent a delegation to the Allied Conference at Spa, to ask for assistance against the Bolsheviks.

Voldemaras himself left Lithuania again in December 1918, but this time under a cloud of controversy. His cabinet had only been formed at the beginning of November, but it was already running into trouble. The government faced severe military difficulties, with Bolshevik troops approaching Vilnius and no significant Lithuanian forces available even to defend the treasury. Voldemaras made some unpopular appointments, particularly that of the Russian General Kondratavičius (Kondratovich) as Deputy Minister of Defence. Kondratavičius attracted much criticism for prioritising the formation of an anti-Bolshevik front comprising all the border states, over the defence of the Lithuanian state.[15] Many of the government's problems seemed to be Voldemaras's personal responsibility since he had appointed himself Prime Minister, Minister for Foreign Affairs, and also Minister for Defence.

On the night of 20/21 December, Augustinas Voldemaras, Martynas Yčas and Antanas Smetona fled Vilnius. Their intentions have been the subject of much debate – while they later claimed that this was a pre-planned trip aimed at securing Western aid, their detractors believed they had deserted their posts. Smetona went to Sweden to raise support for the Lithuanian cause, while Voldemaras and Yčas went to Berlin, where they raised a loan of 100 million marks. In their absence, and with their government discredited, a new government was formed under Mykolas Sleževičius. It was agreed – though without consultation with him – that Voldemaras would keep his position as Minister for Foreign Affairs.

In January 1919 Smetona and Voldemaras toured the Scandinavian countries, canvassing for support.

While Smetona remained in Scandinavia, supervising the work of Lithuanian missions there, in February 1919 Voldemaras went on to London and then to Paris. In London he was interviewed by Rex Leeper, Lewis Namier and James Simpson of the Political Intelligence Department, all of whom were sympathetic to his claims. Namier and Leeper described him as 'an intelligent, level-headed and moderate man ... contrary to the usual habit of the small nationalities he did not unduly exaggerate the ethnic territory of his nation'.[16] Both interviews resulted in long memoranda recounting Voldemaras's points of view, which prompted E H Carr, a junior Foreign Office official who was familiar with Voldemaras, to confess to 'a mild suspicion that some of the views so ably expressed in these 2 memoranda were to some extent suggested to M. Woldemar by the interviewers and that M. Woldemar's share in them was confined to willing acquiescence. Otherwise, at his rate of articulation, these interviews must have occupied a good many hours'.[17]

'He is now on his way to Paris to represent Lithuanian interests at the Peace Conference. He gave us the impression of an intelligent, level-headed and moderate man. Contrary to the usual habit of the small nationalities, he did not unduly exaggerate the size of the ethnic territory of his nation. He admitted that large parts of the Government of Vilna were White Russian and not Lithuanian, and volunteered the information that in the Government of Grodno 71% of the population were Greek Orthodox, who could be nothing but Russians and whom, by no stretch of the imagination, either the Poles or Lithuanians could claim as their own. He admitted that even of the remaining 29% a large proportion are Roman Catholic White Russians. He stated, however, that under present conditions the White Russians of these Governments would readily join the Lithuanians in order to avoid subjection to Poland – a statement which is probably correct.'

Rex Leeper and Lewis Namier on Voldemaras[18]

By the beginning of 1919 Piip, Meierovics and Voldemaras were all representing their countries abroad. They had made valuable contacts in the Foreign Office in London, and had rehearsed the arguments for their countries' independence. Piip and Meierovics, having been there longer, had the best connections. In Piip's case Estonia's military achievements helped him to secure statements of *de facto* recognition; in both cases the plainly anti-German attitude of the Estonians and Latvians helped them to build strong relationships in the West. The first steps had also been taken in co-operation between the Baltic delegates, and this would continue in Paris after the opening of the Paris Peace Conference.

5

The Baltic Delegations in Paris

The Paris Peace Conference was due to open formally on 18 January 1919. Both the Estonian and Latvian delegations arrived in Paris in early January – the Estonians meeting in London on the first of the month and travelling to Paris together, and the Latvians convening in Paris. The official leadership of the delegations was reserved for the older generation of diplomats, Jaan Poska, the Estonian Foreign Minister and former Mayor of Tallinn, and Jānis Čakste who was already in Paris representing Latvia. However, both Ants Piip and Zigfrīds Meierovics had a crucial role to play in their delegations – Meierovics as Latvian Foreign Minister, and Piip as the minister to the country most sympathetic to the Baltic nations (Great Britain), and as a Professor of Law. In addition the Estonian delegation included Nikolai Koestner, the Trade and Industry Minister, Mikhel Martna, a member of the National Council, and Kaarel Pusta, now the Estonian minister in Paris. In the Latvian delegation Čakste and Meierovics were joined by Jānis Seskis. All three were already versed in the arguments for Latvian independence, as they had been working together since the autumn of 1917. The

Latvian delegation was later joined by two left-wing politicians, Felikss Cielēns and Margers Skujenieks.

The composition of the Lithuanian delegation was much more problematic. When Voldemaras left London for Paris in February 1919, there were already at least three focal points for representation. Firstly, Juozas Gabrys, one of the best-known Lithuanian émigrés in the West, had been invited to Paris by the French government, who were strong supporters of the Polish cause, and were pressing for a swift agreement between the Lithuanians and Poles over the territory disputed by the two countries. Gabrys was based in Lausanne, and, as he did not have far to come he was able to arrive in Paris in December. There he took part in conversations with Roman Dmowski, the head of the Polish National Committee, and with Kazimierz Dłuski, who was to be one of the Polish delegates to the Peace Conference. He found it impossible to agree with Dmowski, who advocated annexing large parts of territory claimed by the Lithuanians to Poland. He got on better with Dłuski, who favoured some kind of federation between Poland and Lithuania.

Secondly, the members of the Lithuanian delegation that had been sent to Spa in November arrived in Paris in early January, and presented their credentials. This delegation included Father Konstantinas Olšauskis, the Jewish representative Simon Rosenbaum and the Belorussian representative Dominik Semashko. Thirdly, a group of American-Lithuanian representatives had arrived, who provided much of the finance for the Lithuanian delegation, as well as much-needed practical support and access to unofficial contacts.

All three of these groups were happy to work together, but none had been authorised by the Lithuanian government in Kaunas. The position was about to get even more complex.

Unhappy about Gabrys' involvement, Kaunas proceeded to appoint a peace delegation of its own. This was originally to be headed by Smetona, but as the French government refused him a visa because of his allegedly pro-German tendencies, Voldemaras was instructed to lead the delegation instead. He was joined by Martynas Yčas (who also had no visa but made his way to Paris illegally). Matters were further complicated by Voldemaras's stubborn insistence on presenting himself as the Prime Minister of Lithuania, despite the fact that, as he well knew, this position was now held by Mykolas Sleževičius, who had formed a new government after Voldemaras, Yčas and Smetona fled Vilnius in December 1918. Voldemaras argued that he had not abandoned his post – he was simply representing his country abroad, as its Prime Minister. He was forced to back down after a report was received from Smetona, who acknowledged the Sleževičius government, outlining the new position. Nevertheless, Voldemaras determined the composition of his delegation, including the Spa delegates and the American Lithuanians but excluding Gabrys. Once the Spa delegates and the American Lithuanians had recognised Voldemaras's leadership, Gabrys was left isolated, with no official position.[1]

The chaos in the Lithuanian delegation highlights the difficulties that the Allied governments faced in assessing how far any individual represented who they claimed to. Numerous new small countries were emerging from the former Russian Empire: delegations were present in Paris at various times during 1919 not only from the Baltic states but from Georgia, Armenia, Azerbaijan, the Ukraine, Belarus, the Don and Kuban Cossacks, and from the North Caucasian Government, all seeking admission to the Conference, and audiences with Allied Foreign Ministers. Incidents like the confusion over the Lithuanian delegation did little to enhance their status, though in this case the British Foreign Office seems to have had a pretty clear idea what was going on, both in Kaunas and amongst the émigré groups. However, one problem which dogged both the British and French authorities was their readiness to accept reports of the 'pro-German character' of the various delegates. Olšauskis and the Spa delegates were briefly arrested on their arrival in Paris as they were believed to be German spies. Smetona was denied a French visa on these grounds, and the British Foreign Office received reports on Voldemaras which suggested that it was 'doubtful how far his sympathies are with the Entente'.[2] An MI6 report on the two delegations described Voldemaras as 'an opportunist and untrustworthy in his state-

> 'Professor Woldemar [*sic*] is an opportunist and probably untrustworthy in his statements. His chief opponents at Berne however, Gabrys and Canon Olsevski [Olšauskis], are at least equally open to the same reproach; and have been in the position of irresponsible critics. Both parties have engaged in the same game of playing off Germany against the Entente.'
>
> **MI6 REPORT ON VOLDEMARAS**

ments', but admitted that Gabrys and Olšauskis were 'at least equally open to the same reproach'.[3]

The first objective of all the Baltic delegations was to secure a hearing at the Peace Conference. Both the Estonian and Latvian delegations requested official admission soon after their arrival, but neither was successful. As for the Lithuanians, Olšauskis had already put in a request for a hearing before Voldemaras arrived, but he stopped short of demanding official admittance. He sent the following letter to Balfour, Pichon and Lansing on 23 January 1919.

'We, the Lithuanians, are a small nation. We are a distinct

nation; distinct in breed in language and in culture. We are common only in our human suffering. That we share with all the so-called small, weak peoples, of which we are one. But we small nations have been the cause of wars, many wars.

'Lithuania is one of those lesser states which was the cause of this war. The great powers have [fought] over us, and now some of the greater powers are sitting at a peace conference to deal with our fate as a possible cause of the next war.

'We, the representatives, of the Lithuanian people, ask for a place at this Peace Conference. We do not seek a seat at the table, but we do ask in our pride for standing room back against the wall – where we have stood so long – waiting to be heard when the question of our fate is to be determined. This we do ask on the ground that we are so deeply concerned in our own fate and upon the principle accepted in the armistice which suspended this war: the principle of self-determination.'[4]

When Voldemaras took over the delegation in February he was more ambitious, submitting a letter to the President of the Conference, the French Premier Georges Clemenceau, on 16 February that demanded official admission. He argued that Lithuanian soldiers had fought for the Allies both on the Eastern Front in the Russian Army, and on the Western Front in the American Army. The position of Lithuania *vis-à-vis* the Entente was 'absolutely identical' to that of Poland, and they therefore ought to be given official admission. He saw no contradiction in the fact that Lithuania had not been officially recognised by the Allied Powers – there was clearly a place at the Conference for nations that formed part of another state, such as the British Dominions.[5] Although Voldemaras later claimed that Clemenceau had promised the Lithuanians admittance, he was no more successful than the Estonians or Latvians in this regard.

During the first months of the Paris Peace Conference, the highest decision-making body at the Conference was the Council of Ten, which was composed of the Prime Ministers and Foreign Ministers of Great Britain, France and Italy; the President and Secretary of State of the United States, and two Japanese diplomats. From March this became a Council of Four (the Prime Ministers of Britain, France and Italy, and the President of the United States), with a Council of Foreign Ministers meeting separately. A constantly expanding number of commissions were set up, in which members of the Allied delegations met to deal with individual issues or regions. The opportunities for delegations wishing to be heard were restricted to occasional audiences with the higher decision-making bodies, or with the commissions, and to the submission of memoranda and written proposals. In addition there were numerous opportunities for informal liaison, lobbying, and the exploitation of personal connections. These opportunities were crucial even for officially-recognised delegations. For the Baltic delegations they assumed even more significance, as they had no formal access to the Council of Four or the Council of Foreign Ministers.

As no commission on Baltic affairs was formed until May 1919, the Baltic statesmen had to reconcile themselves to trying to influence the individual Allied delegations and the various inter-Allied decision-making bodies by submitting memoranda and requesting audiences with the individuals most closely involved with decision-making in their area. Sometimes they would get as far as a Foreign Minister but this was not easy. When Meierovics requested an interview with Balfour in June, the Foreign Secretary protested, noting on the request 'Please, I have just spent an hour with an Estonian!'[6] A high point was a joint meeting with Clemenceau on 16 March 1919. Kaarel Pusta and Jaan Poska attended for Estonia, Meierovics and Čakste for Latvia, and Voldemaras for Lithuania. In addition, there were delegates at this meeting from the Ukraine, Georgia, Belorussia, Azerbaijan and the North Caucasian Government. Meierovics asked where, how and when the question of Russia's border states would be dealt with, and when they could finally make their demands known. Clemenceau assured them of his personal sympathy, but stated that the treaty with Germany needed to be settled first, before the Conference could move on to the Russian problem. This meeting lasted a total of 20 minutes.[7]

All of the Baltic delegations developed key Allied contacts with less influence but more specific expertise. Amongst the British, who were certainly the most sympathetic to Baltic independence, important contacts were Sir Esme Howard and James Simpson. Howard, the former British Ambassador in Stockholm who had met both Piip and Meierovics in that capacity, was now the British delegate with responsibility for north-eastern Europe, including Russia, Poland, Scandinavia and the Baltic States. Howard was very sympathetic to the idea of Baltic independence, and was impressed with the 'grit and courage' and amazing 'grasp of actualities in political life' displayed by the Estonian and Latvian representatives. He had less confidence in Voldemaras and his government than the others – perhaps as a result of the confusion surrounding their representation.[8] Simpson, a member of the Political Intelligence Department of the British Foreign Office with responsibility for reporting on Russia's border states, who had met Piip, Meierovics and Voldemaras in London, was brought over to Paris in May. In the American delegation, two key individuals were Robert Lord and Samuel Morison, both members of the 'Inquiry' – the

American unit of academic experts appointed to advise on questions concerning the peace settlement. Lord had responsibility for Polish questions while Morison was in charge of Finland and the Baltic States. He met the Baltic delegates frequently, often over dinner, to discuss their affairs. He had a particularly good working relationship with Kaarel Pusta; perhaps less so with Piip, whom he described as 'a swarthy, excitable little man'.[9]

Samuel Eliot Morison (1887–1976) was a Boston-born historian who studied at Harvard and in Paris. Having worked on Finland for Colonel House's Inquiry, he was seconded from the army to the US delegation at the Paris Peace Conference. His supposed expertise on Finland and the Baltic States brought him appointment as American delegate on the Baltic Commission. He was Harmsworth Professor of American History at Oxford 1922–5, and became full professor at Harvard in 1925. He wrote a 15-volume history of the US Navy in the Second World War and many other works of academic history. He won Pulitzer Prizes for biographies of Columbus and John Paul Jones. He died in 1976.

Esme Howard's diary shows that he also met with Piip, Meierovics and Voldemaras fairly frequently, often over lunch or dinner. They consulted him over the best attitude to take to the proposal that all parties in the Russian conflict should meet at Prinkipo, and he 'advised them to accept [it] on condition of Armistice and recognition of their territory by the Bolsheviks', which is essentially what they did.[10] When the Baltic delegations were granted an audience with a more senior member of the British delegation, Howard was usually involved. The following account gives a flavour of his role, along with an indication of the persistence of the Baltic delegates in arguing their case: 'At 3.15 got a frantic appeal from Ian Malcolm [Balfour's Private Secretary] to go round at once to the Rue Nitot, where the Esthonian delegates were interviewing poor Mr. Balfour, who hated to be alone on these occasions. They were pressing for immediate recognition of independence. They were told – in accordance with the policy at that time – that final settlement could only be with the consent of the Russians. They argued for three and a half hours!' [11]

The demands presented to the Peace Conference by the Baltic delegations shared some broad characteristics. All three wanted military assistance against the Bolsheviks, loans, and recognition – *de jure* in the case of Estonia and Latvia, and *de facto* in the case of Lithuania. They presented their case in extended memoranda to the Peace Conference. Howard described the Latvian memorandum as 'one of the best I have read'.[12]

There were no major territorial disputes between the three Baltic delegations. The border between Estonia and Latvia would be settled relatively easily in 1920, and that between Latvia and Lithuania in 1921. However, since Lithuania bordered both Polish and German territory, some of the territorial demands of the Lithuanian delegation were controversial. Voldemaras outlined Lithuania's claims in a series of letters he submitted to the Peace Conference, on 16 February, 24 March and 29 April. In terms of territory the Lithuanians claimed around 125,000 square kilometres, with six million inhabitants. This comprised the administrative districts of Vilna, Grodno and Suwalki, along with parts of Courland and East Prussia. Voldemaras admitted that this included some areas populated by Belorussians, but stated that these populations had expressed the wish to be part of an independent Lithuanian state.[13] In private conversations some members of the delegation extended their claims into the district of Minsk, but they were disciplined for doing so.

Most controversial were Lithuanian claims to Klaipeda (Memel) and Vilnius. Klaipeda formed a natural outlet to the sea for Lithuania, but had formed part of the territory of the German Empire. The Lithuanian delegation argued that without Klaipeda as their major port, Lithuania would be 'a body without a head' or 'a man deprived of the use of his arms'.[14] Vilnius was the historic capital of the Lithuanian Grand Duchy, a cultural centre for the Lithuanian national movement, and a major centre of trade with a multi-ethnic population. It was also claimed by Poland. In the 1897 census (the last census taken in the Russian Empire) 40 per cent of the population of Vilnius were recorded as being Jewish, 30 per cent Polish, and only 2 per cent as being ethnic Lithuanians. The Poles claimed the ethnographic advantage, and since they also claimed to be the true heirs of Poland-Lithuania, they could also claim Vilnius as historically a Polish city. The situation was thrown into high relief by the fact that the city was the birthplace of Józef Piłsudski, the Polish President and Commander-in-Chief.

A primary demand of all three delegations was for military assistance against the Bolsheviks. The military situation in the Baltic in 1919 was complex. German forces had been in occupation of Lithuania and Courland since 1915 and of the rest of Latvia and Estonia since early 1918. As a condition of the Treaty of Brest-Litovsk, signed in March 1918, the Bolsheviks had conceded Lithuania, Latvia and Estonia to Germany. The German government's intention was that these states would be independent under German influence. However, when the Germans were defeated on the Western Front, the Bolshevik government repudiated the treaty, and Soviet forces began to advance into the Baltic region, capturing Narva and Tartu in November and December 1918 respectively, and Riga and Vilnius in January 1919. The Lithuanian government retreated to Kaunas when Voldemaras fled Vilnius, and Soviet administrations were established in Narva (for Estonia), Valga (for Latvia), and Vilnius (for Lithuania). In Estonia and Latvia these governments were able to work within a structure of home-grown regional soviets, but in Lithuania they were operating in a vacuum. To integrate Lithuania more firmly into the Soviet system, the Lithuanian and Belorussian Soviet Republics were unified.

The Estonian army under Lieutenant-Colonel Johan Laidoner, formerly a Divisional Chief of Staff in the Russian Imperial Army, began a counter-offensive in January. With the assistance of Finnish volunteers and Estonian partisan groups, they drove Soviet forces out of Estonia by the end of February.

In Latvia things were complicated by a relatively high level of local support for the Soviet regime. Pēteris Stučka, who was the putative head of a Latvian Soviet Republic, was a seasoned Latvian Social Democrat politician, with strong connections to the Soviet leadership in Moscow. The Latvian Rifle Brigades were among the most loyal Bolshevik forces, and were a genuinely national fighting force. The nationalist government had no comparable national army – though they were trying to remedy this – and had to rely on external support.

One of the conditions of the armistice was that German forces were required to withdraw from all territory that had been part of the Russian Empire 'as soon as the Allies shall consider this desirable', thus allowing the Allies to use or dispense with these troops as it suited them, and in the Baltic region it seemed that they might be useful in staving off a Soviet invasion. However, the continued German military presence was not fully controllable by the Allies, and over the course of the year 1919 it developed into a formidable problem. After the armistice, German troops in the Baltic were tired and mutinous. They were revitalised by the arrival of General Rüdiger von der Goltz in Liepāja (Libau) in February 1919, as Commander in Chief of all German forces in the Baltic. In combination with the smaller Latvian forces, they began a new phase of attack. They recovered a large part of Latvian territory relatively easily, but in April went on to mount a coup in Liepāja, overturning the Ulmanis government. A puppet government was set up under Andrievs Niedra, with the support of the local Baltic German nobility. Von der Goltz harboured elaborate plans to colonise the area and seize land for his troops. He also hoped for the overthrow of the Bolshevik government so that an accommodation could be reached between Germany and Russia with a view to overturning the Treaty of Versailles.[15] He actively prevented conscription of troops for the Latvian army.

Rudiger von der Goltz (1865–1946) was a German general who was transferred from command of a division in France to lead an expedition to help Finnish Whites expel the Reds from Helsinki in April 1918. Early in 1919 he took control of German and locally-raised Freikorps troops around Liepāja. He drove the Bolsheviks out of Latvia in the spring of 1919, and deposed the Latvian government in Riga in May. After being defeated at Cēsis by Latvian and Estonian forces, he was eventually removed from his command. The Allies found von der Goltz impossible to control and only military defeat by local nationalists eliminated the threat he posed.

At this point the Armistice Commission in Paris ordered the German government to recall von der Goltz and to place all German troops under Latvian command, but when the German force threatened to pull out of the Baltic completely, the Allies had to back down. A combined attack on Riga re-took the city from the Bolsheviks on 22 May, but the Niedra government, not the Ulmanis government, was established there. Concerted action between Estonian and Latvian forces turned the situation around. Estonian troops helped drive Bolshevik forces out of northern Latvia. They then confronted German forces in the Battle of Cēsis, in June. This joint Baltic victory forced the Germans to evacuate Riga, and the Ulmanis government was re-established there in July.

The Lithuanian government faced an equally vexed situation. They were engaged in fighting Soviet forces, which controlled the eastern part of the country, including Vilnius, in the early part of 1919. The Lithuanians had come to an agreement with German forces in the region, and were paying any volunteers who agreed to fight with them – for this reason they were unwilling, initially at least, for the Germans troops to withdraw. The German government supported this policy, as they were unconvinced that the Bolshevik forces would stop at the East Prussian border. Things became increasingly complicated in the spring of 1919 – before the Lithuanian government could retake Vilnius, Polish troops occupied the city. It was feared that withdrawing the German forces would only exacerbate fighting between Lithuania and Poland.

Military assistance was therefore high on the agenda for all the Baltic delegations at the Peace Conference. In a memorandum of 17 January the Estonian delegation asked for arms and munitions, especially artillery, aeroplanes and tanks. Active military support would also be welcomed, in the form of volunteers or regular troops.[16] A list of materials requested, supplied by the Estonian representative in Helsinki, included 20,000 rifles, 2,000 revolvers, 200 machine guns, eight heavy guns, six tanks, 55 automobiles, six seaplanes and over 1,000 kilometres of telephone cable, as well as ammunition, benzine, oil, rubber, field glasses, hammers, thread and chalk.[17] The Lithuanians asked specifically for the transfer of Lithuanian volunteers from the American armed forces, and the withdrawal of Lithuanians from the Polish divisions which had fought on the Western Front. They asked for equipment, ammunition, transport facilities and military missions to assist them with the organisation of the army. Meierovics saw recognition of Latvian independence and Allied military assistance against the Bolsheviks as his two most important priorities. If he could achieve these things, his task abroad would be finished and he would be able to go home.[18]

Financial support was also a priority. The Estonians asked for an Allied loan of £20 million, without which, they argued, it would be impossible to continue the struggle against the Bolsheviks. The Germans had taken 'nearly all resources from the land', and both German marks and Russian roubles were worth so little that it was impossible to raise a loan internally.[19] In a joint meeting with Sir Esme Howard on 15 January, Piip asked for £2 million from the British to raise volunteers in Scandinavia, and to equip Estonian troops; Meierovics asked for £15 million, to be spread over an agreed period, and to be used for defence and reconstruction. In later communications this was broken down into £2 million up front, and £13 million over a longer period – no further assistance would be required.[20] Balfour certainly favoured these loans, on the grounds that they would counter German influence in the region. He asked Lord Curzon, who was running the Foreign Office while Balfour was in Paris, to press the argument on the Treasury.[21]

All three Baltic delegations had to contend with the absence of any coherent Russian policy at the Conference. It was clear from the opening of the Conference that many of the decisions that had to be taken were either dependent on, or would affect, the political situation in Russia. Yet there was no single authority in Russia with whom the Allies were prepared to deal. Herbert Hoover (the head of the American Relief Administration, who accompanied the American delegation to Paris) described Russia as 'the Banquo's Ghost sitting at every council table' at the Conference.[22] James Headlam-Morley, a junior member of the British delegation, recorded in his diary: 'In the discussions everything leads up to Russia. Then there is a discursive discussion; it is agreed that the point at issue cannot be determined until the general policy on Russia has been settled; having agreed on this, instead of settling it, they pass on to some other subject.'[23]

There were several early initiatives to resolve the 'Russian Question', each of which affected the Baltic delegations. On 22 January 1919 the proposal was put forward that all parties in the Russian conflict, including the Soviet government, be invited to a separate peace conference, with Allied representation, on the island of Prinkipo in the Sea of Marmara. The Estonian, Latvian and Lithuanian delegations all accepted this invitation, but with reservations regarding their own right to national independence. Within the Estonian delegation, it was mooted that Piip might be sent as their representative to Prinkipo. The Soviet government also agreed to attend, but the anti-Bolshevik Russians refused, and they were supported in this refusal by reactionary elements in the French Foreign Office and British War Office. Prinkipo was allowed to slide.

A second initiative was the mission sent to Russia under the American diplomat William Bullitt in February to ascertain the conditions on which peace with the Bolsheviks could be secured. Bullitt returned with a proposal, approved by Lenin, that all existing *de facto* governments on the territory of the former Russian Empire should remain in possession of the territory they currently controlled, until the peoples of these territories decided otherwise. None of these governments would attempt to overthrow the others, and neither would the Allies. Although they were not mentioned by name, this document implied Soviet recognition of the legitimacy of the Baltic governments – as did Soviet acceptance of the Prinkipo proposal.

More problematic for the Baltic delegations was the interest which still existed amongst some elements of the Allied delegations in intervention in the Russian Civil War on behalf of the anti-Bolshevik forces. Since early 1918 bitter fighting had been taking place between the newly-formed Red Army and anti-Bolshevik forces led initially by General Alekseev and later by General Denikin in the Caucasus, and by Admiral Kolchak in Siberia. The British and French armies were already offering limited assistance to the 'White' forces, and high-profile figures like Winston Churchill (at this time Secretary of State for War) and Marshal Foch (Supreme Commander of the Allied Armies) were advocating much more substantial military support. The Baltic States benefited from Allied intervention and by the presence of British warships off the Baltic coast. They were also part of Churchill's plan – he wanted to combine the efforts of the independent border states with those of the anti-Bolshevik Russian forces, equipped by the British, to create 'one system of war and diplomacy'.[24] This was never a realistic option, since none of the anti-Bolshevik governments was prepared to recognise the independence of Russia's border states.

In the context of peacemaking in 1919, the ebb and flow of the struggle in Russia created problems. During the spring of 1919, while decision-making in Paris was ongoing, Kolchak achieved a series of impressive victories, capturing Ufa and Kazan, and bringing his forces to within 75 miles of the

Volga. While large-scale Allied intervention was never really on the cards, recognition of Kolchak's government in Omsk began to seem a realistic possibility. In late May the Council of Four prepared a note to Kolchak in which they set out the terms on which they would be willing to continue material assistance to his forces. The note stated that the Allies were disposed to provide munitions, food and supplies to assist Kolchak's government 'to establish themselves as the government of all Russia', but they would need certain guarantees. These included democratic elections in Russia itself, and recognition of Finnish and Polish independence. For the Baltic states the provision was that 'if a solution of the relations between Estonia, Latvia and Lithuania, and the Caucasian and Trans-Caspian territories and Russia is not speedily reached by agreement, the settlement will be made in consultation and co-operation with the League of Nations, and that until such a settlement is made, the Government of Russia agrees to recognise those territories as autonomous and to confirm the relations which may exist between the Allied and Associated Governments and the de facto Governments of those territories'.[25] While the question of diplomatic recognition was studiously avoided in the note, the implication was that it would follow if Kolchak agreed to these conditions, thus proving that his government was truly democratic.[26]

In fact the White challenge to the Bolshevik regime was a chimera. By the end of the year Kolchak had been executed by Bolshevik forces in Vladivostok and Denikin's forces had withdrawn to the Crimea. Unfortunately, Kolchak's successes in the spring of 1919 formed the backdrop to decision-making on Russia in Paris, and blighted Allied Baltic policy at the Conference. The need to take account of Kolchak's government, and the possibility that the anti-Bolshevik forces would win the Civil War, generated a severe contradiction in Allied policy. On the one hand, the British Government in particular was keen to support the independence of the border states, for a number of reasons: to weaken Russia territorially, to develop trade links in the region, and to prevent this region falling under German or Bolshevik influence. On the other hand they had to contend with the likelihood that a restored Russian government, representative of the ally that had fought with them in the war, would not only want its Baltic coastline back, but would object to the actions of the Powers that had removed it. Allied policy was also hindered by the differing objectives of the Powers. Esme Howard described the relations between the Allied delegations as being 'so bitter that they might have been engaged before the armistice in fighting each other instead of fighting side by side'.[27] The result was an incoherent and piecemeal Russian policy on the part of all the Powers at the Peace Conference.

The Baltic delegations had to deal with this while confronting the rival arguments of other delegations with interests in their region. Perhaps the most important of these was the Russian Political Conference, a body formed by the anti-Bolshevik Russian political émigrés to represent their interests in Paris. Chaired by Prince Lvov (former head of the Provisional Government in 1917), its members included other prominent Russian liberals like Vasilii Maklakov, Boris Bakhmetev and Sergei Sazonov. While these anti-Bolshevik liberals had accepted the independence of Poland and in most cases Finland, they had little sympathy for the demands of the Estonian, Latvian and Lithuanian governments. Kaarel Pusta had met Maklakov in Paris back in 1918, and although their relations were cordial, Maklakov had refused to take Estonian independence seriously.

The contributions of the Russian Political Conference to the debate on the Baltic question were generally designed to delay any decision on the independence of the border states. They argued that proximity to Bolshevism was causing the border states to tend towards complete independence, but that no decision on their future could be made without reference to a future restored Russian state, to which their interests were intrinsically linked. They suggested that the Allies allow these provisional regimes to exist, and give them assistance, but that no further decision should be made while the Russian people were unable to participate in the settlement of these questions.[28] This was a genuine and strongly-held belief, and consistent with the views of Piip and Meierovics on the balance of merit between autonomy and independence in 1917. The case the anti-Bolshevik Russians presented was tied to their involvement in the Allied war effort. They had fought alongside Britain and France for three years and sustained enormous losses in men and material. Russia was now suffering from 'the disease of Bolshevism', and needed assistance from her allies. Instead, the Allied Powers were discussing carving up Russia's territory in order to permanently weaken her. As the Council of Four appeared to be considering recognition of Kolchak, the Russian Political Conference reiterated this position in May, with specific reference to the Baltic States – or provinces, as they would have it.

'As far as the three provinces of Livonia, Esthonia and Courland are concerned … their geographical situation binds them especially to Russia. Imperious economic necessity forced the Russian people to sustain a long struggle in order to gain access to the sea. During three hundred years since this purpose has been reached, Russia has made a tremendous effort to develop the ports which are indispensable to her commerce as well as a system of railroads constructed at great expense to carry to these ports a large part of the Russian exports. The Baltic provinces have largely profited by it, for the prosperity of the country is due for a large part precisely to favourable economic conditions resulting from the fact that they were part of Russia. Finally the defense of Russia and of her two Capitals depends largely on the possession of the territories on the shore of the Baltic.

'For all these reasons, Russia will never be able to give up the provinces in question …'[29]

Voldemaras had a doubly difficult job. He had to counter the arguments of the Russian Political Conference, while simultaneously confronting the Polish delegation – not merely on territorial questions, but even on the right of the Lithuanian Republic to exist. The Polish delegates were Prime Minister Ignacy Paderewski, Roman Dmowski, the head of the Polish National Committee, and Kazimierz Dłuski. The Polish delegation and government were divided on the Lithuanian question between federalists and annexationists. The federalists, who included both Paderewski and Piłsudski, had support from the left in Poland but also from Polish land-owners with estates in Lithuania. They favoured a close union with Lithuania, and in some cases were prepared to offer concessions, including Vilnius, to Lithuania in exchange for this. The annexationists, on the other hand, wanted a centralised Polish state, including Vilnius. Despite the fact Paderewski was in favour of federation, and Dłuski was also a supporter of Piłsudski, Dmowski's policy of territorial annexation was the official one adopted at the Conference – perhaps because Paderewski did not arrive until 2 April.[30] Dmowski repeatedly stated that Lithuania would be best served by being linked politically to Poland, as it was too small to be independent on its own account. Many Allied delegates found Dmowski difficult to deal with because of the enormous territorial scope of his claims for Poland.[31] Whatever differences of opinion existed within the Polish delegation, it was united on the Polish claim to Vilnius. The Lithuanians suffered seriously in the first few months of the Conference from the fact that many, particularly in the French and American delegations, tended to see Lithuania as part of the Polish problem. Voldemaras lamented that, since Poland had an official delegation admitted to the Conference, and were therefore able to work more effectively through its structures (being invited to meetings, rather than having to canvass for them), it was likely that the Vilnius question would be seen from their point of view.[32] As unofficial delegates representing unrecognised governments, Piip, Meierovics and Voldemaras faced an uphill struggle in countering the assumptions of the Allied diplomats and the arguments of the Polish and anti-Bolshevik Russian representatives.

6

Baltic Co-operation in Paris

One of the most striking aspects of the work of the Baltic delegations in Paris was the degree to which they worked together, sharing contacts, developing arguments in support of their countries' independence and building a coherent regional identity. This co-operation began in London in 1918. Piip, Meierovics and Rudolf Holsti (the Finnish Foreign Minister) met regularly to share contacts and ideas at the Holborn Restaurant or the Royal Society Club. David Ghambashidze, the Georgian representative in London, was also part of this circle. It was perhaps only the friendship of Piip and Holsti that enabled Meierovics to keep up his morale in the face of social isolation and severe financial hardship.[1]

Voldemaras only arrived in London in February, and was not part of this group. By then Piip and Meierovics were already in Paris. Nevertheless, co-operation between the Estonian, Latvian, Finnish and other delegations continued in Paris, and the inclusion of the Lithuanians in this circle was a natural process. They attended meetings together, such as that with Clemenceau in March, and issued joint declarations – a phenomenon which began early in the Conference, and continued to the end. On 19 April 1919 the Estonian, Latvian, Lithuanian, Georgian and Ukrainian representatives joined together in a declaration asking for a hearing to discuss recognition and admission to the Conference.[2] Towards the end of the Conference, on 6 September 1919, the Estonian, Latvian and Lithuanian delegations wrote a joint letter to the President of the Peace Conference expressing their 'complete solidarity' and common aspirations, and asking for a decision to be taken as soon as possible on the recognition of their independence.[3] Nonetheless, their rhetoric on independence differed in some important ways, and the Lithuanian delegation remained slightly apart from the others.

The Estonian and Latvian demands for recognition of their independence were based on the ethnic coherence of their new states. Both Piip and Meierovics were firm believers in the rights of small nations to self-determination. Their memoranda on this subject exploited the current Wilsonian ideology, and argued that they had the same rights as any other self-defined nation. They drew attention to the high level of education and advanced cultural and literary development of their countries, and played on the chaos and anarchy in the region: their governments represented stable elements capable of restoring order. Responding to the Russian Political Conference's assertion that no questions regarding the territory of the Russian Empire could be decided without Russian participation, the Estonian delegation argued that, as an independent nation, they could not be expected to rely on the acquiescence of another people in determining their future status. Nor would waiting for a democratic Russia be in the interests of world peace. Estonia had a stable government now, and needed recognition in order to attract loans from other countries and consolidate its internal situation further.[4] Similarly, a Latvian memorandum drawn up in February 1919 argued that delaying recognition would mean anarchy rather than order. They played on both the rhetoric of national self-determination and the Conference's top-down decision-making structure, stating that they were 'sure that the Peace Conference is competent to make final decisions on the status of these new States, in collaboration with these States, without making its decisions contingent on Russian consent. The Peace Conference has already applied this principle to Poland.'[5]

Both the Estonian and Latvian delegations were ostentatiously willing to establish friendly relations with a restored Russian state, and to allow their neighbour access to the facilities of which it was feared Baltic independence might deprive them. From the beginning of the Conference, the Estonians stated that their policy would be 'the complete freedom of transit and use of Estonia's free harbours', while the Latvian delegation promised 'reasonable economic concessions with a view to facilitating free access to the Baltic Sea for [Russia]'. At the same time they strove to adopt the tone and language of already independent nations – especially since the Russian Political Conference insisted on speaking as an Allied Power, 'reserving the right to decide' on the fate of the Baltic nations. In response to the Russian note in May, Meierovics set out a series of demands relating to the repatriation of Latvian nationals, and the right of any Latvians in Russia to choose between Russian and Latvian citizenship. Latvia was an independent state, dealing with another state.[6]

The Lithuanian position was somewhat different. Voldemaras wrongly believed that the Lithuanians had a strong hand to play at the Peace Conference, since Lithuania had a long history as an independent state, and did not have to rely only on ethnographical arguments. The inclusion of Rosenbaum and Semashko, the Jewish and Belorussian representatives, in the Lithuanian delegation, was intended to strengthen this position. Voldemaras saw the question of access to the Baltic Sea as affecting only the Estonians and Latvians, and having no practical economic or strategic implications for Lithuania's independence. He was adamant that Lithuania would not return to Russian domination: during the period in which they had controlled Lithuania the Russian authorities had systematically destroyed the culture and economy of the country. They had proved incapable of protecting Lithuania from German invasion, and had devastated the country during their withdrawal. The Poles, equally, had a history of exploiting Lithuania for their own ends. Since independence the Poles had behaved aggressively towards Lithuania as towards all their neighbours. Voldemaras dismissed the idea that an independent Lithuania would be open to attack because of her size, stating that in this new era of international relations it was not the size of nations that would guarantee security, but the League of Nations, of which Lithuania wished to be a member.

Even as independent states defined by their ethnic coherence or historic basis as a state, Estonia, Latvia and Lithuania faced the problems consequent upon geography and size. Notwithstanding elements of sympathy in the Allied delegations, more traditional military and strategic minds were sceptical of the independence of three such tiny states. Sir Henry Wilson, the Chief of the Imperial General Staff, when discussing the future of Estonia and Latvia with Sir Esme Howard, directed him to a map of Russia and commented: 'Look at those two little plots on the map and look at all that enormous country beside them. How can they hope to avoid being gobbled up?'[7]

An effective response to this, with broad appeal within the Allied delegations, was the concept of the Baltic states as part of a '*cordon sanitaire*', or 'barbed-wire fence', between Germany and Russia. It was natural for rhetoric on Baltic independence to centre on defining the new independent countries against the foreign 'others' that had dominated them in the past. For Estonia and Latvia particularly, but also for Lithuania, the German occupation was a natural focus, and the memoranda submitted to the Allies by all three delegations contained numerous references to German oppression and the opportunities to thwart German plans and extend Allied influence by supporting the independent national governments. Defining their identity against the Russian Empire had not been a major part of the rhetoric of any of the Baltic national movements before 1917. It was the Bolshevik Revolution that shaped appeals on this side: the motifs of anarchy, violence and destruction associated with the Bolshevik regime were used to good effect in contrast with the order and moderation of the national governments.[8]

'Look at those two little plots on the map and look at all that enormous country beside them. How can they hope to avoid being gobbled up?'

SIR HENRY WILSON ON ESTONIA AND LATVIA

In the absence of domination by Russia or Germany, a new orientation developed around the idea of a Baltic League. In many different manifestations, this concept became an important part of Baltic rhetoric on independence, developing through discussions between the Baltic delegates and sympathetic Allied diplomats. As early as the autumn of 1917 the issue had been raised by Jaan Tönisson, the leader of the Estonian Progressive People's Party, at a special session of the Estonian Maapäev which had been called to address Estonia's military and political position following the German capture of Riga. A number of familiar possibilities for Estonia's future had then been discussed: a state within a Russian federation; union with Germany; complete independence. Tönisson's assessment of the bargaining power of the Baltic states in international circles was interesting. 'With a German victory in the Baltic Sea, the English would be excluded from the Baltic Sea ... England would never consent that the Baltic area remain under Germany. For that reason it should be possible to create a buffer state from the Baltic lands by reconciling the conflict of interest of the great powers ... if the Lithuanian, Latvian, Estonian, Finnish, and Scandinavian people unite, they would have, as a union of thirty million people, a certain amount of influence during the negotiations at the Peace Conference. In the same way as with England, the general interest of the United States would also coincide more or less with the interests of the Baltic-Scandinavian people.'[9]

At the time this idea stemmed from the fact that, while a Russian federation seemed to be less likely in the face of the growth of Soviet power in Russia, complete independence for the three Baltic states was still not seen as a viable possibility. Pre-war diplomatic rhetoric had made the independence of small European states seem anomalous, and Baltic politicians were aware of their weakness.[10]

But notions of what such a Baltic League might mean, or what political combinations around the Baltic Sea were possible, or desirable, differed widely. Jaan Poska, the Estonian Foreign Minister, defined the Baltic Sea region as comprising three distinct areas – Scandinavia, the Eastern Baltic and the Southern Baltic.[11] On this basis Ants Piip and Kaarel Pusta drew up a memorandum which outlined a system of interlinked alliances: first between Norway, Denmark and Sweden;

secondly between Finland, Estonia and Latvia; and thirdly between Lithuania and Poland. This triangular league would possess a common armed force and a co-ordinated navy, and would act as one on political and economic questions.[12] One of Meierovics' chief objectives in going to London had been to establish co-operation with the other Baltic representatives, and he became one of the strongest champions of the idea of a Baltic League.

The Estonians and Latvians tended to align themselves with Finland, partly because of their strong relationship in these matters with Holsti, but also because of the cultural ties between Finland and Estonia, and the more secure status of Finland as an independent state. The Lithuanians would not consider any kind of alliance with Poland, as in all Polish rhetoric on this Poland was considered to be naturally the dominant partner. There were Lithuanian advocates of an alliance with Estonia, and particularly Latvia – Dr Jonas Šliupas was a notable example – but Voldemaras often seemed reluctant to tie his country more closely to the Estonian and Latvian cause. His conviction that Lithuania occupied a special and more defensible position as an independent state because of its history did nothing to help Lithuania's integration into this regional identity in the minds of Western diplomats. Before his arrival in Paris he spoke in quite negative terms to Simpson about Latvian independence – using the arguments about access to the Baltic Sea, but also drawing attention to the Latvian interest in a Russian federation in 1917 and to the sympathy of the Latvian population for Bolshevism.[13] Associating Lithuania with the emerging Baltic regional identity would have been tactically useful for Voldemaras, in the face of challenges to Lithuania's existence from both the Polish and Russian delegations. If they were associated with it, however, it was more often through the efforts of individuals like Piip and Meierovics.

Allied diplomats also took an early interest in such projects, which fitted in with the general vogue for federative schemes for international co-operation in the post-war period. Francis Lindley (British Chargé d'Affaires in Petrograd), writing to Balfour after meeting the Estonians for the first time in 1918, expressed the view that they would be best off as an autonomous entity in a Russian federation, but if this proved impossible they should be independent and 'form a block with Scandinavia, Finland and perhaps Poland'.[14] Esme Howard was perhaps the chief British protagonist of the Baltic League. He had looked favourably on closer co-operation between the Scandinavian countries, and saw this new proposal as a way of encouraging unity and stability under British influence in a part of Europe where British interests were insecure. Although it would be unlikely to have any real military power, the League could function as an economic bloc and as a diplomatic unit speaking 'with one voice' at international congresses. Howard advocated a leading role for Sweden; he hoped this would 'flatter the vanity' of the Swedes and draw them away from Germany. To this end he argued against the inclusion of Poland, as Sweden might resent the presence of another larger power, and the Lithuanians would certainly be unhappy about their involvement.[15]

Schemes for a Baltic League were also designed to appeal to the pragmatism of the British and French governments, in creating a barrier between Germany and Russia, and providing opportunities for economic expansion in the Baltic. There were regular references to the idea of a *cordon sanitaire* in memoranda to the Peace Conference. As early as January 1919 the Estonian delegations invoked the idea of the 'creation of [a] sanitary cordon, as proclaimed by Allied public opinion' which could be supported by Allied military and material aid.[16] The Latvians also drew attention to the possibilities presented by the Baltic States as a force under neither Russian nor German domination in the region – a barrier not just against Bolshevism, but preventing a Russo-German alliance.

However, while the idea of supporting the independent Baltic States as a *cordon sanitaire* against both Bolshevism and against German expansion had a certain appeal, it ran contrary to the prevailing mood in Paris, which was conditioned by Admiral Kolchak's military successes in the spring of 1919. The prospect of the anti-Bolshevik Russians winning the Civil War and re-establishing the Russian Empire made Western observers much more wary of acknowledging the independence of parts of its former territory.

In the meantime, it was the Estonian delegation, rather than the Lithuanians, who tended to be looked on the most favourably. This was in large part because of their military achievement in pushing the Bolsheviks out of their territory, but also because of their plainly anti-German stance. Most of the discussions which related to the Baltic States in the early part of the Peace Conference were concerned with providing them with material support. If recognition was raised, it was usually in the context of guaranteeing supplies or loans to the Estonian, and sometimes the Latvian, government. The Food Section of the Supreme Economic Council (a body formed in February 1919 to advise the Peace Conference on economic issues) questioned in April whether these states were going to be recognised, and if so, whether one or more Allied Powers would take the responsibility for assisting them financially and with supplies.[17]

In a meeting of the Council of Foreign Ministers on 9 May, Balfour brought up the question of granting *de facto* recognition to Estonia, in order to encourage the Estonians in their fight against Bolshevism. Britain, of course, had already done so, and Stephen Pichon acknowledged that the French government were treating the Estonians as a *de facto* government. However, Robert Lansing, for the American delegation, interpreted this as a significant policy step that he was not prepared to take. 'The recognition of *de facto* governments in territories formerly Russian, constituted in a measure a dissection of Russia which the United States of America had carefully avoided, except in the case of Finland and Poland. In the case of Poland Russia herself had acquiesced.' [18] Balfour dropped this point, since he was more interested in securing material aid for the Estonians than arguing about recognition. The United States were providing a considerable amount of food aid in Estonia (and Herbert Hoover said so at this meeting), but could not provide financial assistance as they did not recognise the government. Italy was unwilling to advance anything. Balfour was particularly keen that financial aid should be given as a small amount would make a huge difference. Pichon was also willing to explore this, but both he and Balfour would have to seek permission from their governments (and particularly from the Budget Committee of the Chamber of Deputies, and the Treasury).

Provision of food aid to Riga was also discussed at this meeting – the problem being that since the Latvian Ulmanis government had been overturned, the only authority capable of distributing food and ensuring that it did not fall into the hands of the Bolsheviks were the Germans. The British navy could deliver food to Riga, but both Pichon and Balfour found the suggestion of Lansing and Hoover that they co-operate

ANTONIUS PIIP, ZIGFRĪDS MEIEROVICS AND AUGUSTINAS VOLDEMARAS

with the Germans to restore order in Riga completely unacceptable. For Lansing the Allies were already effectively allied with the Germans in the Baltic States since they had asked them to remain there. He was also in possession of accounts of German activity in the Baltic States wholly at odds with the reports Balfour was receiving: the latter thought that the Germans had been 'behaving disgracefully in the Baltic provinces and were acting for their own political ends', while Lansing believed that von der Goltz was 'behaving with considerable good faith', and that 'there existed no danger of German misbehaviour'. American concerns were primarily humanitarian: 'even if the Germans were devils in Hell the people should still be fed'.[19] This conflict pushed the Council of Foreign Ministers to establish a committee of military and naval representatives 'to report on the best means of keeping and maintaining order in the Baltic States and revictualling the population' – one of two 'Baltic Commissions' – the first decision-making bodies at the Conference to deal directly with questions concerning the Baltic region.

7

The Baltic Commissions

In April and May 1919 the Council of Four and the Council of Foreign Ministers began to direct more attention to the discussion of Baltic affairs. Reports were reaching Paris on the activities of the German troops still in the region, particularly von der Goltz's coup in Liepāja, and an Allied decision on whether these troops should be ordered to withdraw was becoming more urgent. The result was the establishment of two separate Commissions on Baltic Affairs – one initiated by the Council of Four and one by the Council of Foreign Ministers. On 16 April 1919 President Wilson put forward to the Council of Four a proposal from Robert Lord, the American specialist on Polish and Baltic affairs, that a commission of enquiry should be sent to the Baltic States 'to study on site the questions relating to the establishment and future of Finland, Latvia, Estonia, etc'. This suggestion was accepted by the other Allied leaders.[1] However in a further discussion on 28 April they decided (again on Lord's recommendation) that, as each power already had representatives in the Baltic region, it would be more useful for the commission to meet in Paris.[2]

THE FIRST BALTIC COMMISSION (14 MAY 1919)

Herbert Hoover (1874–1964) was the head of the American Relief Association, and a member of the Supreme Economic Council. He organised relief programmes across Eastern Europe in the aftermath of the war. Hoover became Secretary of Commerce under Warren Harding in 1921, and became President of the United States himself in 1929.

William Shepherd Benson (1855–1932) was Naval Advisor to the American Peace Delegation. An Admiral in the US Navy, he had acted as Naval Representative in the Allied War Councils in 1917–18. He retired from the Navy in 1919, and during the 1920s served as Chairman of the US Shipping Board.

Colonel James Addison Logan (1879–1930) had been Chief of the US Military Mission to the French Army between 1914 and 1917, and became an Assistant Chief of Staff in the American Expeditionary Force in 1918. In 1921 he became an adviser to the American Relief Administration. He retired from the US Army in 1922.

Sir Esme Howard (1863–1939) was the member of the British Peace Delegation with responsibility for Northern European Affairs. He had been Ambassador in Stockholm during the war, and continued his diplomatic career after the war as Ambassador in Madrid, and later Washington.

Sir William Goode (1875–1944) was Director of British Relief Missions and a member of the Supreme Economic Council. He had been a journalist, working for the Associated Press, the *Standard* and the *Daily Mail* before 1914, and during the War he worked on a series of relief and military organisation committees. He later became an unofficial financial adviser to Hungary, and during the Second World War was chairman of the Council of British Societies for Relief Abroad.

Admiral George Price Webley Hope (1869–1959) was Deputy First Sea

Then, at the meeting of the Council of Foreign Ministers on 9 May, another Baltic Commission was proposed, this time at the suggestion of Balfour. This commission was to be made up of Allied delegates each with military, naval, economic or political expertise: Herbert Hoover, Admiral

Lord in 1918–19, and was present at the signing of the armistice in November 1918. He commanded the 3rd Light Cruiser Squadron in the Mediterranean in 1921–3, and retired from the British Navy in 1926.

General William Thwaites (1868–1947) was Director of Military Intelligence at the War Office 1918–22. In the inter-war period he was involved with the Territorial Army, commanding the 47th (2nd London) Division in 1923–6, and was Director-General of the Territorial Army in 1931–3. He retired in 1933.

Jacques Seydoux (1870–1929) was an economist at the Quai D'Orsay, and had been one of the architects of the Allied blockade policy during the War. He became the head of the Commercial Relations Department at the Quai D'Orsay in the 1920s, dealing with reparations, inter-Allied debts, and the restoration of trade. He was a hugely important figure in French diplomacy and policy making.

Admiral Ferdinand-Jean-Jacques de Bon (1861–1923) was a member of the Inter-Allied Naval Council of the Peace Conference. He had been on the General Staff of the French Navy since 1913, and Chief of the General Staff since 1916. He died in office in 1923.

Alphonse-Joseph Georges (1875–1951) attended the Peace Conference as a member of Marshal Foch's staff. He had served on the Western Front and in Greece during the War and was made Colonel in December 1918. In the inter-war period he took part in the occupation of the Ruhr and sat on the Dawes Commission. He commanded operations in the north-east of France at the outbreak of the Second World War. He fled to Algiers in 1943 and became a member, with De Gaulle, of the Committee of National Liberation.

Mario Grassi was a Rear-Admiral in the Italian Navy. He was later one of the signatories of the Treaty of Trianon.

Benson and Colonel Logan for the USA; Sir Esme Howard, Sir William Goode, Admiral Hope and General Thwaites for Great Britain, and M. Seydoux, Admiral de Bon and Colonel Georges for France. Rear-Admiral Grassi represented Italy. These individuals were tasked with addressing the problem of 'maintaining order in the Baltic countries and ... delivering foodstuffs to their population'.[3]

Despite being brought into existence later, Balfour's Commission was the first to meet. It convened on 14 May at the Ministry of Commerce. The members of the Commission concluded that the maintenance of order was a necessary precondition to sending foodstuffs to the Baltic States, and that, as it was impossible for the Allies to send troops to the region, and the current situation of relying on the Germans was not satisfactory, the only option was to encourage the organisation of the local forces, along with any available volunteers. To this end, they made six recommendations.

1. In accordance with Article XII of the Armistice the Germans will be required to withdraw from Latvia and Lithuania as soon as they can be replaced by local organised forces but must remain where they are until orders are issued. The organisation of local forces should be carried out with the least possible delay.

2. A competent Military Mission under British Command to be organised under a Lieutenant or Major-General with Headquarters at Libau or Reval, for the purpose of advising the Governments of Estonia, Latvia and Lithuania on questions of organisation, equipment and training of all local forces and such volunteer forces as may be raised from external sources. The Mission to be appointed for the purpose of advising the Governments aforesaid on the best means of defence against the Bolsheviks and for the exclusion of the Germans from their territories.

3. Volunteer forces mentioned in (2) to be raised by voluntary recruitment in the Scandinavian States, including Finland.

4. A credit of £10,000,000 to be placed at the disposal of the

Baltic States by the Allied and Associated Governments and to be applied as required under the arrangements of the political and military missions.

5. Food supplies, equipment, clothing, arms, munitions, etc., to be supplied by the Allied and Associated Powers, the cost being defrayed from the credit referred to in (4).

6. It will be the duty of the political and economic missions to see what collateral securities can be obtained from the three Baltic States, to cover the credit referred to in (4) wholly or in part.[4]

When they discussed this report on 23 May the Council of Foreign Ministers agreed on points 1, 2, 3, 5 and 6. Point 4, since it required a large monetary advance, was referred to the Council of Four, along with a question prepared by Balfour as to whether an Estonian advance on Petrograd, and Petrograd itself, should be supported with food aid, and whether Kolchak should be consulted about this; and a seventh recommendation put forward by Lansing (but disliked by the others, particularly Balfour), suggesting that 'the Director General of Relief should continue to extend *ravitaillement* in all non Bolshevik areas of the Baltic region without respect to political control'.[5] The proposed military mission departed for the Baltic in June.

The Council of Four's Baltic Commission met on 15 May. In all it met on 22 occasions between May and September 1919. It was chaired by Sir Esme Howard, and the Marquis della Torretta, the former Italian ambassador in St Petersburg, acted as vice-chair. The American representative was Samuel Morison, the French representative was Henri Kammerer – head of the Russian Bureau in the French Ministry of Foreign Affairs – and the Japanese representative was Ketato

Otchiai, the Japanese minister to the Netherlands. In later meetings of the Commission E H Carr took over from Esme Howard, and Major Royal Tyler from Morison.

At the first meeting, on 15 May, there was extensive discussion of the remit of the Commission, particularly in the light of the existence of the other Baltic Commission which had met the previous day. Esme Howard had its recommendations to hand, and his fellow Commission members approved these. They forwarded a resolution to the Council of Foreign Ministers supporting the proposal to send a military mission to the Baltic States, and also asking Allied representatives in Liepāja to assist with the creation of a coalition government in Latvia.[6]

Both Howard and Kammerer agreed that the remit of their own Commission was much wider, and should take in all questions relating to the countries of the Baltic – their internal condition, external relations and particularly whether they should be considered to be independent states, whether some form of federation or alliance between them were possible, or whether they should be considered simply as provinces of Russia, but with considerable autonomy. They agreed they would hear the delegations of each country concerned, and although they could not invite a Russian delegation to speak, they would invite individual Russians, as was the practice on other commissions.[7] However, this question was revisited on 22 May, as the Italian delegate, della Torretta, had been absent and was concerned at the lack of direction received from the Council of Four. He was unhappy that the Commission should carry on its work on the vague and extremely wide programme outlined at the first meeting, as the existence of the Commission was well known, and while the Estonians and Latvians believed their independence was about to be recognised, the Russians felt threatened. The Commission risked arriving at conclusions, particularly on the question of the integrity of Russia, which ran completely contrary to their governments' policies.[8]

Howard made these points in a letter to Maurice Hankey, the Secretary of the British delegation, and told him that the Commission would continue its work on Baltic affairs, but would not consider the relationship between the Baltic States and Russia until they were authorised by the Council of Four to do so. He stressed that the recent successes of Admiral Kolchak seemed to make his recognition by the Allies a matter for serious discussion, and that consideration should be given to the question of assurances to the Baltic provinces in this case. At a meeting on 24 May, the Council authorised the Commission to examine the future relations of the Baltic States with Russia.[9]

Della Torretta was right in his observation that the existence of the Baltic Commission was exciting great interest and extreme concern amongst all the delegations with interests in the region. During the course of its meetings the Commission provided a platform for Estonian, Latvian, Lithuanian, anti-Bolshevik Russian and Baltic German representatives to make their case. It also heard reports from Allied experts who had first-hand knowledge of events in the Baltic. While the selection of individuals to speak in front of the Commission depended to some degree on the availability of people in Paris with relevant knowledge, the order in which the various delegations were heard was indicative of the significance attached to them. Vasilii Maklakov, a member of the Russian Political Conference, was heard on 26 May; Ants Piip, Kaarel Pusta and Nikolai Koestner of the Estonian delegation were heard on 28 May; Zigfrīds Meierovics and two other Latvian delegates were heard on 10 June; and Voldemaras and the Lithuanian delegation not until 7 July.

All the members of the Commission began from a position of sympathy for the Baltic delegations. At the first meeting, Howard made clear his own opinion on the position in each of the three Baltic States. The Estonians, he stated, had an impressive record of military opposition to the Bolsheviks, but were desperately in need of financial assistance. In the case of Latvia, the question of how far the population should be considered Bolshevik had to be considered before deciding whether to give local forces Allied support. Howard personally believed that Bolshevik sentiment in Latvia was purely a result of the German occupation (as the major landowners were also German), and that swift land reform measures on the part of the democratic government would sort this out. The situation in Lithuania was more complicated, but he considered it less important – it could be left on one side for the moment. Although Kammerer still thought that Estonia, Latvia and Lithuania had little in common, Howard argued that their common desire for freedom from both Russia and Germany united them, and that this made schemes for a federation involving the three states viable.

In Maklakov's interview on 26 May, he repeated the Russian Political Conference's line that the fate of these nationalities could not be decided definitively without the consent of the Russian state. He did not believe there was any genuine separatist feeling amongst the populations in these states – their desire for independence stemmed simply from the need to dissociate themselves from the anarchy of Bolshevik rule. The Provisional Government had, after all, united Estonian territory and given the Estonians a national assembly. This could not be done for Latvia as most of their territory had been occupied by Germany in 1917. From the point of view of a restored anti-Bolshevik Russia, the complete independence of these areas would be ruinous both strategically and economically. It would also be difficult for the Baltic States to manage on their own without Russia's resources to draw on – they had benefited in the past from Russian investment in railways, and Russian trade through their ports. When pressed by the committee he stated that their attitude to Lithuania was exactly the same as to Estonia.[10]

The Estonian delegation was granted an audience on 28 May, in order, as Howard put it, 'to report on the situation in Estonia and acquaint us with your wishes'.[11] Ants Piip and Kaarel Pusta did most of the talking. Piip asserted the desire of the Estonian people for complete independence, which had been proclaimed in February 1918 and reaffirmed by the democratically-elected Estonian Constituent Assembly in April of that year. He pointed to the assurances that had already been made to the Estonians by the Allies, and stressed that there was no need to wait for the constitution of a new Russian government, which would only attempt to deny the Estonians the right to speak for themselves. He stated that Estonia hoped for financial and economic aid from the Allies, but most of all swift recognition, without which they could not take responsibility for the military situation or for internal order.[12]

Pusta concentrated on the Estonian contribution to the War. Estonians had fought loyally on the Allied side, he argued, and more recently had fought both Germans and Bolsheviks, with small, poorly armed forces. All this proved the will of the Estonian people. Pusta compared Estonia to other states which had now received recognition for their contribution to the War – Poland, Yugoslavia, Czechoslovakia, and Finland. Like these nations, Estonia wanted recognition and admission to the League of Nations. Both men stressed that their government envisaged good neighbourly relations with Russia, and was prepared to grant Russia free access to the Baltic, if necessary under the control of the League of Nations. In fact, just as Estonia had acted as a barrier to the spread of the Russian anarchy, the country could now act as an open door to the civilised world, facilitating the resumption of relations with Western Europe.[13]

Howard replied that the British Government intended to honour the assurances it had given to Estonia. He was obliged to add, however, that it was difficult to decide the status of the Baltic provinces without agreement with Russia. The absence of an established government in Russia explained the hesitation of the Allied and Associated Powers. Kammerer and della Torretta expressed their agreement for the French and Italian delegations, and supported Howard when he expressed the Commission's deep admiration for the heroic struggle the Estonian people had undertaken against the Bolsheviks, with manifestly insufficient means. Piip ended by reinforcing the position that, although Estonia had once been part of Russia, it was not now, and no new Russian government would have the right to speak on its behalf. Without Allied recognition the continued struggle would be more difficult, as it would be hard to keep up morale in the army and the population.

The sympathy of the members of the Commission for the Estonian predicament was clear. Nevertheless, the logic they applied to this predicament was always based on the assumption that there would ultimately be a restored anti-Bolshevik government in Russia. After Piip, Pusta and Koestner had left, the members of the Commission indulged in a lengthy discussion about the level of autonomy or independence they envisaged according to Estonia within a Russian federation, taking in the questions of customs, defence, the monetary system, and citizenship. It was an almost pointless debate, ignoring the fact that there was no liberal Russian government for them to deal with; it also overlooked the fact that if there were, and they considered Estonia to still be a part of Russia, then they would have little say in any of these decisions. The only way the Commission could actually reach concrete conclusions was to agree that they did not consider Estonia to belong to a Russian sphere of influence.[14]

It was 10 June before the Latvian delegation were received, and in the meantime the exchange of notes between the Allies and Admiral Kolchak had taken place. When the meeting opened, and while Meierovics and the other delegates waited outside, della Torretta again raised the question of the remit of the Commission. He had nothing against hearing the Latvian case, he said, since this had long been promised. But given the negotiations that were ongoing with Kolchak's government, he felt that the Commission no longer had the power to decide the future constitution of Latvia. Otchiai, the Japanese representative, agreed that the Commission's work had less authority in the light of the exchange of notes regarding recognition and support for Kolchak's government. Kammerer and Howard, on the other hand, whose governments had made assurances of various kinds to the Baltic delegations, felt bound to continue with their work. They eventually talked the members of the Commission round, arguing that their work could at least be seen as a preparatory exercise, potentially of use to the League of Nations later.[15]

The Latvian delegation was finally allowed into the meeting. Meierovics had submitted two memoranda, and he was invited to address verbally the points within them. In the first of these he, like the Estonians, played on Latvian sacrifices in the War, which he stated they had borne 'in the name of the high principles inscribed on the banner of the Entente against the imperialism and militarism of Germany'. They had 'sacrificed everything for world democracy, civilisation, humanity and the freedom of Latvia', and were still fighting for freedom against their neighbours, Germany and Bolshevik Russia. Meierovics quoted statements by the former French Ambassador in Russia, and the British, Italian and Japanese Foreign Ministers expressing their sympathy with the Latvian cause, and said that he was sure the Allies would confirm their recognition of Latvia at the Peace Conference.[16]

The second note dealt with Latvia's external relations. Meierovics demanded recognition of Latvia as a sovereign independent state, 'one and indivisible' (in a nice play on the rhetoric of the Russian Political Conference). All borders with neighbouring countries should be settled on ethnographical lines, with any adjustments necessary to the economic lives of the countries concerned. Where there was a dispute it should be settled by an international tribunal, or the League of Nations, which Latvia hoped to join. Latvia's interests were completely opposed to those of Germany, but neither could Latvia be regarded as part of a pan-Russian question. He recognised Russia's need for access to the Baltic Sea via Latvian ports, and was happy to accommodate this as long as it did not threaten Latvian sovereignty. Meierovics stated that Latvia was prepared to take on a fair proportion of the Russian national debt as it stood prior to the Bolshevik seizure of power, providing that Russia paid compensation for the destruction and removal of Latvian property by its troops. In addition all Latvian nationals in Russia should be allowed to return to Latvia, and they should have the right to choose whether they wanted Latvian or Russian citizenship. Meierovics drew particular attention to Latvia's good relations with Finland and Estonia to the north, and Lithuania, Belarus and Poland to the south, and emphasised the many interests they had in common. In order to counter the tendency towards Russo-German rapprochement (which was evident at the moment in the co-operation of Germans, Baltic Germans and Russians in intrigues in Latvia), he intended to develop Latvia's existing alliances with these neighbouring states, and asked the Peace Conference to grant them the liberty to do so. Latvia was now almost entirely clear of Bolshevik forces, and it was only the German occupation that was causing a problem. Therefore he asked for the immediate evacuation of German troops, as well as the repatriation of Latvian soldiers from Siberia, Germany and France.

As with the Estonian delegation, Howard confirmed the assurances of *de facto* recognition that had already been made, pending the decision of the Peace Conference. He assured Meierovics that the Allies were very much in sympathy with the desire for liberty of the Estonian and Latvian people. But he also stated, as with Piip and Pusta, that it was almost impossible to recognise the independence of these countries without the consent of the Russian government, which the Commission was convinced would soon be re-established. Howard pointed out that the Allies were actively concerned with the situation at the moment. Meierovics emphasised his request that the future of Latvia should be an international question, not dependent on the decisions of the Russian constituent assembly. He hoped that 'you will yourselves find the best solution to relations between Latvia and Russia'. At that point Howard thanked the delegation and promised to give the questions they had raised 'scrupulous attention'.[17]

In fact after the Latvian delegation had left the Commission did not discuss any of the issues that had been raised, moving on instead to other questions. When Meierovics submitted another memorandum to the Commission on 16 June, dealing with the actions of German troops in Latvia and asking for their immediate withdrawal, its receipt was noted by the Commission but no reply was given – as Kammerer put it, 'we can't respond to all these Latvian notes, there are really too many of them'.[18]

> 'We can't respond to all these Latvian notes, there are really too many of them.'
>
> **HENRI KAMMERER**

The Baltic Commission received a request for a hearing from the Lithuanian delegation on 19 May, but this request was not granted until 7 July. It was clear from their discussions that the members of the Commission, even the most sympathetic like Howard, saw the Lithuanian government as less stable, less trustworthy and less inclined towards the Western Allies than the Estonians and Latvians. Nevertheless, the fact that the Lithuanian delegation was heard by the Baltic Commission at all can be regarded in some respects as an achievement, as it demonstrated that the Allies were moving towards considering them as part of a 'Baltic question' with Latvia, Estonia and even Finland, rather than as part of a purely 'Polish question'. Their inclusion along with Estonia and Latvia in the note to Kolchak in May also marked a clear shift in this direction. Both Voldemaras and Yčas had been invited in late April to speak to a subcommittee of the Commission on Polish Affairs, but had refused as they had been invited only as individuals familiar with Lithuanian affairs, not as representatives of a Lithuanian government. They wanted to be heard in their own right. When they did speak to the full

Polish Commission on 10 May, they demanded recognition of Lithuanian independence.[19] Their hearing at the Baltic Commission suggests that by the summer of 1919 it was at least possible for Lithuania to be regarded in Allied plans as part of a regional unit with Estonia and Latvia.

The Lithuanian delegation that was seen on 7 July was led by Voldemaras, but contained members who had recently arrived in Paris from Kaunas – Justinas Staugaitis, Vice-President of the Kaunas government, Canon Grigaitis, Colonel Gedgaudas, a member of the Lithuanian General Staff, and Petras Klimas, the Secretary of the Taryba. Under prompting from Howard, Staugaitis gave the committee a comprehensive account of the current internal situation in Lithuania. He stated that order was now almost completely established in the country. A government was established in which all the major political parties were represented, along with the Jewish and Belorussian minorities. All but the Polish minority were in favour of an independent Lithuania. Unfortunately in the current conditions it had been impossible to hold elections to form a parliament. The government had an army which was repulsing foreign invasion and maintaining order in the interior without help from other troops. Under normal circumstances the government would be able to support itself perfectly well on its own resources, but of course was having to equip and feed an army, and cope with the fact that the Germans were carrying off moveable resources like timber.

On the German question, Voldemaras pointed out that the Lithuanian delegation had submitted a request to the Conference that the Germans be evacuated from their territory. They offered little protection and posed a threat to internal order. They were also expensive – up to this point the Lithuanian government had been paying them 4 marks each per day. When

Colonel Warwick Greene, also attending this meeting, raised the issue of anti-Polish and anti-Semitic sentiment in Lithuania, Voldemaras dismissed the latter at least, pointing out that the Lithuanians had traditionally formed a bloc with the Jewish parties against the Poles in the Imperial Duma elections.

Summing up, Howard was able to present a surprisingly favourable picture of the Lithuanian situation: there was a national government representing all parties, it could keep order with its own forces once the Germans were gone, and organise enough local forces to defend the border against the Bolsheviks. The economic situation was not as bad as in the other Baltic states, and the Lithuanians did not need urgent food supplies. They had plenty of materials to export – they just needed credits for their army. In thanking the Lithuanian delegation, Howard stated that the Committee wanted to help their country to form, like the other Baltic States, a stable government and to maintain a barrier against German influence on one side and Bolshevism on the other. He said that a decision could not be taken at the moment but would be as soon as agreement was reached with Russia. Without that a durable peace was not possible. He also stated that it was important to avoid all conflict with the Jewish population and to reach an amicable settlement with the Poles. He hoped a solution would be found on the question of a loan.[20]

The Commission had also interviewed Baron Meyendorff, acting as a representative of the Baltic German populations, on 17 June. In his presentation to the Commission he argued that the grievances held against the Baltic Germans, and the actions of some of them, should not lead to the condemnation of all Baltic Germans. They, like many Russians and Latvians, had to seek protection from the Bolsheviks by co-operating with the Germans. Military co-operation did not necessarily indicate political co-operation. He was the first to deplore the recent German actions in Latvia, but he believed that Latvia's efforts against the Bolsheviks were being hampered not only by German activity but also by the appeal of Bolshevism in Latvia. In his opinion it was not desirable that immediate evacuation should take place, and it was not possible for a national Latvian army to be immediately formed. He also criticised what he considered to be arbitrary measures to redistribute land belonging to Baltic German landowners. These people had done a lot for the country in terms of improving the land and production. Most Baltic Germans were pro-Kolchak and in favour of continued union with Russia; they did not anticipate long-term independence for the Baltic countries.[21]

The Baltic Commission spent a lot of time during the spring and summer of 1919 on the issue of the evacuation of German troops from the Baltic region and whenever there were Allied experts in Paris with knowledge of affairs in the Baltic region they were brought before the Commission. When the Commission had first addressed the issue, in the middle of May, they had been of the opinion that there was no need to order the recall of German troops from Latvia, provided that von der Goltz, their commander, was given clear instructions that he should facilitate the construction of a coalition government in Latvia, rearm the Latvian troops, and make no attempt to impede the formation of local forces.

Although aware of the German coup in April against the Ulmanis government in Liepāja, the Commission underestimated its importance. The Commission's opinion on the situation in Latvia changed as news began to filter through of the nature of German activities there: the installation of the Niedra puppet government in Riga, and the threat of a German advance into Estonian territory. On 22 May the Commission heard from Major Keenan, just back from Liepāja. He reported on the situation since the coup d'etat, and stressed the necessity of re-establishing the Ulmanis government, and forming a Latvian army as soon as possible.

On 10 June Howard met with Ants Piip and Kaarel Pusta, who were 'much agitated, poor people, about [the] German attack on Estonia'. Howard was now convinced that the Germans must be required to evacuate the Baltic region, but regarded this as 'a hopeless situation' – it was difficult to suggest a 'practical way of inducing them to do so'.[22] At a meeting of the Baltic Commission the same day, a recommendation to the effect that the German government should be asked to withdraw its troops from Latvia was drawn up, to be put in front of the Council of Four. The Council accepted this recommendation on 12 June, and communicated this message to the German government the following day.[23] This position was reinforced by the evidence of Colonel Greene, head of the American mission in the Baltic, who had returned to Paris from Liepāja, and spoke to the Baltic Commission on 17 June. Greene brought with him a joint declaration from the British, French and American missions in the region, pointing out the acute danger posed by German troops moving north from Riga towards Estonia. Greene stressed the necessity of granting credits to the Baltic governments, perhaps in exchange for guarantees of timber and flax. He also urged the speedy appointment of an Allied military mission. This had in fact already been appointed, and had left for the Baltic.[24]

The Allied military mission, led by the British General Sir Hubert Gough, arrived in Latvia in the middle of June. The mission docked in Liepāja before going on to Tallinn (Reval) and establishing relations with the Estonian Government and military. Gough also met Marshal Mannerheim in Helsinki, and made it clear (as he had orders from Curzon to do) that the British Government would not support a Finnish attack on Petrograd. Gough was unclear what the brief of his mission actually was, but spent most of his time dealing with the Germans in the region, whom he felt represented a far larger problem than the Bolsheviks.[25] He was unhappy with the plethora of Allied representatives in the Baltic. At least three other missions were already present, and there was no organised chain of command through which Gough could issue orders. Besides the American mission that had been led by Greene, there was a British economic mission in Latvia, under Stephen Tallents (previously an official in the Ministry of Food, and later Secretary of the Empire Marketing Board), and a French military mission in Kaunas, led by Colonel Reboul. This mission had been there since March – apparently with the underlying objective of promoting union between Poland and Lithuania.[26] Gough was anxious for all these missions to operate through him, and to convey a single message to the German command in the Baltic. However, as Sir Henry Wilson pointed out, the only orders that von der Goltz would obey were those of Berlin, and the only person who could give orders to Berlin was Marshal Foch.[27] Gough felt that supporting the independence of the Baltic States was 'the only sensible and realistic policy at that time'.[28] Writing to Henry Wilson he said 'There is no question in my mind what our policy ought to be in the Baltic – 1) Get rid of the German

'There is no question in my mind what our policy ought to be in the Baltic – 1) Get rid of the German troops 2) support the provinces and open trade with them 3) drop the Russians!'

GENERAL SIR HUBERT GOUGH

troops 2) support the provinces and open trade with them 3) drop the Russians!'[29]

The withdrawal of German forces from Lithuania remained more complicated. The Commission were happy that the Lithuanian army was holding its own against the Bolsheviks, but were concerned that German withdrawal would exacerbate existing tensions between Lithuanians and Poles in the region. The Commission wanted the withdrawal to be accomplished in such a way as to avoid the occupation of these areas by Polish forces.[30] At a meeting on 13 June, a report from the French military mission in Kaunas was considered. On the basis of Colonel Reboul's assessment of the territory controlled by the Lithuanian government the Commission set a demarcation line between the Poles and Lithuanians to be maintained on German withdrawal. This left some territory regarded as Lithuanian in Polish hands, and vice versa, but the line was not intended to prejudge any final settlement. The Commission's decision was telegraphed to Reboul in Kaunas and General Gough in Estonia.[31] However, when Polish forces moved beyond this line during June and July, Foch proposed a new line, supported by the Commission on Polish Affairs, which effectively acknowledged the new position.[32]

A problem that emerged during the course of these discussions was the issue of German removal of rolling stock from the region. The German administration in the Baltic had converted the region's railways from the Russian broad gauge to the German gauge during the war, and the removal of rolling stock would make distribution of food aid very difficult. The Commission agreed a letter to the Council of Four stating that the German government must be asked to leave the rolling stock as a form of compensation. They also urged that the railway gauges be changed back, as it would be better for the Baltic States to be well connected to Russia than to Germany. An additional problem was the apparent reluctance of the German troops to withdraw at all. The Baltic Commission submitted a further memo to the Council of Four on 3 August urging the importance of speeding up the evacuation – a second resolution on the subject was issued by the Supreme Council on 15 September.[33]

The need for some formal clarification of Allied policy on the Baltic was clear to the members of the Baltic Commission from the outset of their work. In each of their interviews with the Baltic delegations they had made it clear that no decision could be made on recognition before the wider Russian question was settled, but there was nevertheless an expectation that the Baltic Commission would make some sort of recommendation, or statement, on how these relations should be worked out. They had been authorised by the Council of Four to do this on 24 May. They were prompted to renew their discussions on this issue by Esme Howard at a meeting on 2 July.

Howard brought two documents to this meeting. The first was a letter from the Estonian delegation, presented to him by Kaarel Pusta. In it Pusta stated that if the Peace Conference found it impossible to recognise Estonian independence, it must refer the question on to the League of Nations or another international body for consideration, and pending such a decision, Estonia should be considered a *de facto* independent state. The second document was a draft declaration, drawn up by Howard himself, on Allied policy on the Baltic States. His intention was to clarify Allied policy to the governments of these states, to the Russian Political Conference, and to Kolchak. His declaration stated: 'The Allied and Associated Powers recognise once again as *de facto* independent the Governments of Estonia and Latvia, and for the first time the Government of Lithuania; they affirm their decision to assure these states of the free self-government desired by their populations.' It went on to say, however, that the Allied and Associated governments were of the opinion that it was not possible to arrive at a definitive solution without the consent of a recognised Russian government. They hoped for a solution satisfactory to all parties, but could not take any further measures towards a definite solution until there was a re-established Russian government.[34]

In view of the facts on the ground this statement was reasonable and cautious, but it was still disputed by other members of the Commission: each approached the declaration from the position of their own government. Detailed discussion of the text was reserved for their next meeting, on 4 July, giving each member of the Commission a chance to consult with his delegation. Kammerer, for the French, was fairly happy with the tone and content of the declaration, but pointed out that the French government had previously recognised the Estonian National Council as an 'independent body', but not a government. Otchiai said that his country had recognised the Estonian and Latvian governments as *de facto* independent bodies, but was not willing to extend this to Lithuania. Tyler pointed out that the US government had not recognised any of them *de facto*, and 'according to the instructions I have received, it has no intention of doing so'. In fact as Della Torretta pointed out, the US government's position was more complicated than this. It had admitted the *de facto* existence of the Baltic governments in the Allied note to Kolchak when they had spoken of the relations that existed between the *de facto* governments of these territories and the Allies. Under challenge, Tyler agreed to submit the declaration to Lansing to see if he would approve it, but reported back on 7 July that this approval had not been forthcoming.[35]

E H Carr, who replaced Esme Howard on the Baltic Commission from 11 July, attempted to advance this declaration. In order to make it acceptable to all the Allied delegations, all references in the declaration to the Baltic 'states' were removed and replaced with 'territory' or 'populations'. Although the American member of the Commission (now Colonel Greene) could still not accept the declaration, it was nevertheless adopted and sent to the Supreme Council as a suggested declaration to be sent to the Baltic delegations and to be copied to the Russians in Paris and to Kolchak. The text eventually read as follows:

'The Allied and Associated Governments have the strongest desire and will to do everything in their power to assist the Baltic governments in the organisation of their defences and in the establishment in these regions of stable and organised governments, with a view to general peace. They furthermore declare their intention to protect their freedom in the event that a centralised and strong government is installed in Russia.

'At the same time it seems to them impossible to arrive at a definitive solution, guaranteeing a durable peace without prior arrangement with a recognised government in Russia; and while reserving the right to contribute, be it directly or by means of the League of Nations to an arrangement satisfactory to both parties, they cannot at present take any step that binds them to a definite decision before the restoration in Russia of a recognised government.'

The declaration had a rough ride at a meeting of the Supreme Council on 26 July 1919, and the question was adjourned, throwing the members of the Baltic Commission into despair over the prospect of continuing their work.[36] By 20 August, however, the situation had changed – the Council was keen to issue some sort of declaration to the various Baltic States, and asked again for a draft declaration. The Commission agreed that there was little point issuing any note within the boundaries that had been set for them. After all, the governments of the Baltic States did not want to be assured of their autonomy, they wanted independence. Carr suggested that they add in some practical measures, such as recognising these governments' passports, official represent-atives, and flags, which might give them some satisfaction. They could also give Lithuania *de facto* recognition, which they had already done for Estonia and Latvia. He presented a new draft which was agreed and sent to the individual Allied delegations.[37] When it was eventually considered, the British, Japanese and Italians gave their approval, but Major Tyler had again to report that 'the Delegation of the United States cannot in the circumstances recognise these states as inde-pendent *de facto* bodies. It does not believe that the time has come to make a declaration on this subject'. The draft was therefore not sent to the Supreme Council.[38]

E H Carr and the British delegation found this whole process deeply unsatisfactory, since the British Government had long since made much more explicit statements on Baltic independence, particularly to the Estonians.

'At the time these assurances were given it was doubtless the intention of HMG at the Peace Conference to support the recognition of the provisional independence of the Baltic States and as late as May the British Delegation were still in favour of recognising Estonian independence, subject to certain guarantees for the preservation of Russian interests. I still think that such recognition would have been more expedient, more equitable and more in accordance with the pledges given by us than any other solution. The assurances given to Estonia undoubtedly had the result of creating the impression that we were prepared to support Estonian independence at the Peace Conference and gave valuable encouragement to the Estonians in the fight against Bolshevism.

'This being the case it is unfortunate that the other delegations, especially the American, appear to be firmly set against any form of recognition of the Baltic States and will not go in any way outside the words used in the Note to Admiral Kolchak.'[39]

Esme Howard also left the Peace Conference disheartened. He felt he had argued 'in season and out of season, that we should assist the Finns, the Baltic States and the Poles to obtain all requisites in food and clothing, in equipment in arms, ammunition and instructors for the formation of the best possible organs of defence'. The border nationalities were 'strong in their new-found liberty, and I believed would fight like men inspired in defence of that liberty'.[40] Nevertheless, he was pretty doubtful about his own influence on policy at the Peace Conference. 'Whatever I proposed or suggested to help the nations adjacent to Russia against Bolshevik attacks met with a stony

> 'The assurances given to Estonia undoubtedly had the result of creating the impression that we were prepared to support Estonian independence at the Peace Conference and gave valuable encouragement to the Estonians in the fight against Bolshevism. This being the case it is unfortunate that the other delegations, especially the American, appear to be firmly set against any form of recognition of the Baltic States and will not go in any way outside the words used in the Note to Admiral Kolchak.'
>
> **E H CARR**

silence. Though I was head of the Department whose business it was to deal with the present condition of Russia and which had collected a mass of evidence on the situation, I cannot remember that I was once asked to discuss with the Prime Minister any single matter connected with Russia and her attitude to her neighbours. Whether he read any of the Memoranda and reports we sent in I cannot tell. I really wondered what use I and my excellent helpers Carr and Palairet could be in these circumstances. It was singularly disheartening never to hear even a word of criticism of our reports.'[41]

The Commission on Baltic Affairs had given Piip, Meierovics, Voldemaras and their delegations a platform to appeal to some of the most sympathetic members of the Allied delegations. However, the existence of the Commission also stifled their opportunities for less formal negotiation. The need for all the delegations to agree on the precise wording of the declaration to the Baltic States resulted in the final draft being almost meaningless – and even this mild statement was not acceptable to the Council of Four, who sought to avoid making any definite statements on Russia. Some of the measures recommended by the Commission were readily adopted by the Council of Four: the need for the withdrawal of German troops, and the requirement to leave behind the rolling stock, for example. Others were ignored, as in the case of the draft declaration, or even reversed, as with the Lithuanian-Polish demarcation line. The questions of recognition and relations with Russia seemed impossible for the Allied delegations to reach agreement on, and this resulted in the progress of the Baltic States towards recognition reaching a standstill, and even moving backwards, during the life of the Baltic Commission.

Russian and Baltic policy had always been low on the

agenda at the Paris Peace Conference, but nevertheless a great deal of work continued to be done in Paris after the signing of the Treaty of Versailles on 28 June 1919. This was despite the departure from Paris of some of the key individuals involved in work on the Baltic question. Howard's last meeting as chair of the Baltic Commission was on 7 July, and he left Paris soon afterwards. Simpson had also left in early July. The Baltic delegates themselves had to make decisions about whether their presence was still required in Paris or whether more useful work could be done at home. Voldemaras and Yčas returned to Lithuania in the middle of September, although the Lithuanian delegation was not formally broken up until December 1919, after another brief visit to Paris by Voldemaras.[42] Meierovics left Paris on 3 July, leaving Jānis Seskis in charge of the Latvian delegation.[43] The Estonians discussed disbanding their delegation on 9 July, and Poska returned to Tallinn on 16 July. Although Piip seems to have remained there for some time longer, he was back in Estonia by the autumn.

The Treaty of Versailles did contain some references to Baltic affairs. Articles 28 and 99 stipulated that the Germans should evacuate Klaipeda and the area surrounding it, and made provision for Allied occupation of this area until its future could be decided. Article 87 postponed the settlement of Poland's eastern frontiers. Article 116 annulled the Brest-Litovsk agreements. Article 117 obliged Germany to respect future Allied treaties with the countries of the former Russian Empire. Lithuania was referred to in Article 433 as an existing but not established government. None of these provisions were definite decisions – they postponed the settlement of Baltic questions to be dealt with by the League of Nations, or, more often than not, by military and political developments in the region.

8

Settlement of Territorial Questions, and Recognition

Allied attempts to bring about the withdrawal of German troops from the Baltic States dragged on in Paris and in the Baltic region through the autumn of 1919. Local military intrigues and central government intransigence meant there was little active response to the Allied demands for a German withdrawal. Following the Battle of Cēsis (21 June–3 July 1919) in which combined Estonian and Latvian forces defeated German forces, von der Goltz was obliged by the Allied missions in the region to sign the Treaty of Strazdumuiza. General Gough required the Germans to evacuate Riga by 5 July, and to effect a general evacuation within an agreed timeframe. This was not the end of Freikorps activity in the Baltic, however. Encouraged by the German authorities in East Prussia (who were very hostile to the Versailles Treaty and assumed that no German government would ratify it) and by local Baltic German landholders, von der Goltz and his troops did everything they could to avoid giving up their position in Latvia. The aim for many of these individuals was to win the right to remain in the Baltic after the War, and to colonise the area, but they also thought of involvement in an anti-Bolshevik campaign in the direction of Petrograd.

Both von der Goltz and the German War Minister, Gustav Noske, held talks with anti-Bolshevik Russian politicians in Berlin, on the possibility of combining their efforts. While some troops that had performed badly at Cēsis were sent home, new recruits raised in Germany were transported to Latvia via East Prussia. Pavel Avalov-Bermondt was chosen by the Germans to lead units of anti-Bolshevik Russians (the 'West Russian Army') which were being formed around Jelgava, 40 kilometres south-west of Riga, and the German troops prepared to join these troops in an offensive against the Bolsheviks which would also neutralise the national governments in the Baltic. The Weimar Government was not opposed to individual soldiers joining the anti-Bolshevik Russians on a voluntary basis, but stated that they must choose either to join the Russians or return to Germany. Events spiralled out of even von der Goltz's control when, after being ordered to entrain for Germany in August, members of the Freikorps mutinied, refusing to leave. In September they were transferred to Avalov-Bermondt's command, so that von der Goltz was nominally no longer in charge of them and could not comply with demands to send them home. At the beginning of October these forces, led by Avalov-Bermondt, began to move from Jelgava towards Riga.[1]

In response to the persistent violations of their orders to evacuate the area the Supreme Council decided, in a meeting of 10 October 1919, to create yet another inter-Allied military commission, this time specifically aimed at overseeing the evacuation of the Baltic provinces. This was headed by the French General Niessel, and included British, American, Italian and Japanese representatives. Niessel had clear orders that the evacuation was to include not only German units, but also individual German soldiers who had been taken into Russian units. No rolling stock or supplies were to be removed from the region by the troops. Niessel's commission left Paris for Berlin on 5 November, and returned on 16 January 1920. They met with Noske in Berlin, with other military figures in Königsberg, and finally with General von Eberhardt, who had taken over the command from von der Goltz, in Tilsit. Eberhardt tried to circumvent and delay the evacuation. He argued that German troops under Russian command had taken Russian citizenship and were therefore no longer his responsibility. At one point he even used the process of evacuation to seize control of the railways. It was only under the pressure of attacks by both Latvian and Lithuanian forces that Eberhardt eventually agreed to remove his troops by 15 December. The agreement specified that all materiel would be left in place, but when the troops did eventually retreat around the middle of that month they looted and burned everything in their path.[2]

The settlement of territorial issues also dragged on beyond the end of the Paris Peace Conference. The two most controversial issues remained Vilnius and Klaipeda, both of which were claimed by the Lithuanians. The Lithuanian government had been based in Vilnius until January 1919, when the city fell to Bolshevik forces. Voldemaras had fled abroad and Sleževičius reorganised the government in Kaunas. The occupation of the city by Polish troops in April 1919 was a severe blow to the Lithuanians, forestalling any serious possibility that they might recover it. Vilnius had always been a multi-ethnic city, and the Lithuanians could not base a claim to the city on the 1897 census. Nevertheless, the Lithuanian delegation in Paris had consistently argued for recognition of the Lithuanian state with its capital in Vilnius. Although the Polish population was larger, at around one-third of the city's population, they did not have a majority either. Around 40 per cent of the city's inhabitants were Jewish, and this added to the importance of the good relations established by Voldemaras's delegation with Jewish-Lithuanian representatives. Of course, all claimants were prepared to count the Jewish population in or out of their community when it suited them.

In actual fact the phenomenon of a large non-Lithuanian city-dwelling population was replicated in Kaunas, which was situated in indisputably Lithuanian territory. Most industrial workers there were either Polish or German, not Lithuanian, and the Russian government had made it difficult for Lithuanian intellectuals to find government posts in Lithuanian cities. The ethnic Lithuanian population tended to live in the countryside, or emigrate. At the Peace Conference, however, an ethnographic advantage was important. Lithuanian arguments on this issue tended to centre on data from either side of the 1897 census – either emphasising earlier statistics from the 1860s which showed a majority of 'Lithuanians' living in the city, or highlighting the fact that the Lithuanian national awakening only reached Vilnius in the early years of the 20th century. In 1897, therefore, Vilnius's inhabitants may have been less likely to describe themselves as 'Lithuanian'.[3] Voldemaras's own justification for the Lithuanian claim ran as follows: *In claiming Wilna as the capital of Lithuania we take account of three principles, ethnographical, economic and historical. In the case of the ethnographic principle we do not think merely of its linguistic aspect. In the town of Wilna you will find 100% of the population who can speak Polish, but you distinguish between English and Americans although they speak the same language, and also between the Finnish and Swedish elements in Finland. As a matter of fact, Helsingfors is more Swedish than Wilna is Polish. It is not enough to speak Polish to be a Pole, and our contention is that very many of those in Wilna who speak Polish are Lithuanians.*

'I think that Lithuania is impossible as an independent state without Wilna, because it is the centre of our intellectual and economic life. It stands on a knot of railways and lies to-day well within the ethnographic boundary.'

AUGUSTINAS VOLDEMARAS

Again economically, I think that Lithuania is impossible as an independent state without Wilna, because it is the centre of our intellectual and economic life. It stands on a knot of railways, and lies to-day well within the ethnographic boundary.[4]

No decision was taken on the question of Poland's eastern frontiers at the Paris Peace Conference. The only decisions taken with regard to Vilnius had been the fixing of the demarcation line by Colonel Reboul on 18 June (based on the Baltic Commission's decision of 13 June), and the later 'Foch Line' of 26 July. Both left Vilnius under Polish control. These demarcation lines were intended simply to stop skirmishes between Polish and Lithuanian forces, not to indicate any kind of final settlement. A further line, the 'Curzon Line' was fixed in December 1919, but this again left the question of Vilnius undecided. Despite repeated suggestions that the Vilnius dispute would be settled by the Supreme Council, the issue was resolved, initially at least, by the events of the Polish-Soviet War which broke out in the spring of 1920.

During the negotiations for peace between Lithuania and Soviet Russia in the summer of 1920, the Soviet Government offered to restore Vilnius to the Lithuanians if they agreed to the passage of Soviet troops through their territory. This was controversial, as Polish forces were in retreat from this area, and had in fact been willing to hand the city over to the Lithuanians rather than letting it fall to the Bolsheviks. The passage of the Red Army through Lithuanian territory also exposed the government to intrigues on the part of the Lithuanian Communist leader Vincas Kapsukas. A Polish retreat from Vilnius but final victory in the war was probably the best outcome that the Lithuanian government could have hoped for. Peace between Lithuania and Soviet Russia was signed in July, and the Red Army handed Vilnius over to Lithuania in August. The Lithuanian government officially declared Vilnius their capital on 26 August 1920. Lithuania also gained control of the surrounding districts, with a population of nearly half a million.

Under pressure from the League of Nations, the Polish government acknowledged the new *status quo* and signed a treaty to that effect in Suwalki on 7 October 1920. However, only two days later the Polish General Żeligowski seized the city, along with territory assigned to Lithuania by their peace treaty with Russia, including Trakai, Lida and Grodno. This area was governed by a commission of Poles led by Żeligowski, and was given the title 'Central Lithuania'.

In May 1921 talks on the issue opened at the League of Nations. Paul Hymans, the former Belgian Foreign Minister, was assigned the task of mediating between delegations led by the Lithuanian and Polish representatives to the League, Ernestas Galvanauskas (the former Lithuanian Prime Minister), and Simon Askenazy. Attempts to secure an invitation for representatives of Żeligowski's administration to these talks were rebuffed. The Lithuanian delegation came to Geneva prepared to negotiate close economic relations, access to the Baltic for Poland, and even joint defence agreements, in return for Polish recognition of the independence of Lithuania, with Vilnius as its capital. Hymans' plan went much further, however, recommending that Lithuania be constructed as a federal state in two parts (Kaunas and Vilnius), and tying Polish and Lithuanian foreign, defence and economic policies together. Needless to say this arrangement was not acceptable to either side, but nevertheless both delegations adopted the strategy of agreeing on this arrangement as a basis for discussion, and then attempting to alter it. For the Lithuanians the fact that the plan acknowledged Vilnius as the capital of Lithuania made it a viable point to work from, even if it was unacceptable in many other ways. However, this policy did have its risks – no Lithuanian government could afford to publicly renounce its claim to Vilnius, and Galvanauskas was the victim of an assassination attempt when he seemed to be considering the Hymans plan too seriously.

When Hymans produced a second draft in August 1921, the Lithuanians stuck to their strategy of agreeing to it as a basis for discussion, but this time the Poles rejected it outright. Although it was endorsed by the League Council, Hymans' proposals had little influence on the realities on the ground in Vilnius. In January 1922 elections to an assembly for the Vilnius district were held, using boundaries which maximised the representation of Poles at the expense of Lithuanians. While the Polish populations participated enthusiastically, the Lithuanian and Jewish populations abstained. The newly-elected Provincial Assembly passed a resolution on 20 February 1922 in favour of uniting these districts with Poland. This was ratified by the Polish parliament in the spring, despite protests from the Lithuanian government and from the League of Nations.

The Treaty of Versailles removed the Klaipeda region from

Germany, but did not give it to Lithuania, essentially because of the uncertainty surrounding Lithuania's future position. None of the Allied governments were yet willing to formally recognise Lithuanian independence, and were therefore reluctant to award territory officially to that state. Nevertheless, the general assumption at the Paris Peace Conference appears to have been that Klaipeda would eventually be awarded to Lithuania, whether as an independent state, part of a Russian federation, or in some sort of union with Poland. When the issue had been discussed by the Baltic Commission in Paris, Kammerer had commented that this area would 'without doubt be given to Lithuania', but he did not believe that the Lithuanian government were at that time in a position to administer it.[5] When the German delegation protested against the loss of the region, Clemenceau wrote to them as President of the Peace Conference saying that the region 'had always been Lithuanian', and that the fact that the majority of the inhabitants of the town of Klaipeda were German 'could not justify leaving the entire territory under German sovereignty, particularly because the port is Lithuania's sole exit to the sea'.[6]

The Baltic Commission had recommended to the Supreme Council that an inter-Allied force of around 5,000 French and Italian troops should be sent to occupy and administer the region until a decision could be taken on the issue. There was some discussion about whether the evacuation of German troops from Lithuania ought to be completed before such a force was sent, but as M. Laroche, one of the French representatives pointed out, there was no better way to speed up the German evacuation than to send Allied troops to Klaipeda.[7]

Klaipeda remained under Allied control until 1923, during which period uncertainty continued over whether the territory would eventually be handed over to Lithuania. The British Government was in favour of recognising Lithuanian independence, assigning Klaipeda to Lithuania, and cultivating Baltic regional co-operation. However, the French administration in Klaipeda, led by Gabriel Petisne, was quite pro-Polish and envisaged handing the area over to some kind of Polish-Lithuanian federation. There was also a strand of thinking which tended towards keeping Klaipeda under League of Nations control, as a 'free state' like Danzig. The issues of Vilnius and Klaipeda seemed to become increasingly linked in Geneva. In early 1922 the British put forward a proposal, which the Lithuanian government rejected, to give Lithuania Klaipeda, *de jure* recognition and some economic aid in exchange for giving up their claim to Vilnius. The Lithuanian Foreign Minister at the time, Vladas Jurgutis, refused outright, saying: 'There can be no question of such a barter – both territories are ours!' [8]

In Lithuania the government increasingly tended towards taking the matter into its own hands. Jonas Zilius, Lithuanian representative in Klaipeda from 1922, advocated a Lithuanian military take-over of the area, which he believed could be achieved within 24 hours. The model was the Polish coup in Vilnius, which had been accomplished smoothly and with little League of Nations intervention. To further the scheme, the Lithuanian government bought up property in the region, gained control of sections of the press, and financed pro-Lithuanian organisations there. To counter Polish and French opposition, they sought the tacit agreement of the German and Russian governments before making any move. While preparing the coup, the government learned that a French-led committee appointed by the Conference of Ambassadors (an inter-Allied body intended to oversee the fulfilment of the peace treaties) was going to present a report on the future of Klaipeda on 10 January 1923. It seemed likely that this would be unfavourable to Lithuania. On 9 January – a day before French troops marched into the Ruhr – around 1,000 Lithuanian troops marched into Klaipeda, establishing control fairly easily. The incident was presented as a local uprising. The French, who had lost men in holding the territory on behalf of the Allies, were the only ones to protest vociferously. The Polish government did not consider the Lithuanian seizure of Klaipeda significant enough to allow tensions between Poland and Lithuania to escalate. The Conference of Ambassadors protested formally, and discussed sending more Allied troops to the region, but eventually decided to acknowledge the transfer – even thanking the Lithuanians at one stage for helping to bring about a peaceful solution to the question.[9]

The boundaries between Estonia and Latvia, and Latvia and Lithuania, were settled without much difficulty. As a result of the contacts that had been made during 1919 both in Paris and in the Baltic region, British representatives were brought in to oversee the settlement of both borders. In early 1920, Stephen Tallents, head of the British Economic Mission, and later British Commissioner in the Baltic States, headed a commission to decide a dispute on the Estonian-Latvian border over the town of Valga. Tallents' decision to award the bulk of the town to Estonia, but a small part, to be used as the nucleus for a market, to Latvia, caused much consternation amongst the two governments and in the local press. One cartoon depicted Tallents as a modern-day Solomon, cutting the town in half; another popular tale held that one house in the town had been bisected, and that its owner now slept with his head in one country and his feet in the other. Tallents, in view of his newly-elevated position, was reluctant when asked to take part in the resolution of a dispute on the Latvian-Lithuanian border.[10] He recommended that whoever took on the job, it should be someone who would not have to stay in the Baltic after they had given their verdict. In consultation with the British Foreign Office, James Simpson, who had had much contact with the Baltic delegates at the Paris Peace Conference, was suggested.

The main points of contention between Latvia and Lithuania were the ownership of Palanga, a coastal town on the border between the two countries, and two railway 'triangles' at Mazeikiai and Kalkuone. As communications in Tsarist times had been constructed with the needs of the Russian Empire in mind, railway hubs existed in either country which were of vital importance for communication between cities and ports belonging to the other. The issue of Palanga was complicated by the ongoing confusion over ownership of Klaipeda. Although Simpson pressed the British Government on this, he was forced to make a decision without any insight into how that issue would be resolved. He awarded Palanga to Lithuania, on the grounds that although it was not a port, it was the closest thing to a viable trade outlet available. He recommended that a convention on the use of railways be drawn up by the two countries, in order to designate the railway triangles as 'exchange points' to be used as required by both Latvia and Lithuania. The Lithuanians were broadly satisfied, and named a street after Simpson in the newly-acquired town of Palanga. The Latvians complained that Simpson's decision was excessively favourable to the Lithuanian government. Meierovics, despite good relations with Simpson, expressed his strong dissatisfaction with the decision. A demonstration against the border settlement was organised in Riga, but was eventually called off after public statements from Simpson that he would 'rather cut off his right hand than harm Latvia'.[11]

The question of peace and the settlement of boundaries between the Baltic States and the Soviet Union was raised while Piip and Voldemaras were still in Paris. On 31 August 1919 Georgii Chicherin, the Russian Foreign Minister, made a radio broadcast inviting the Estonian government to open peace negotiations to determine the border between the two states. If the Estonians did not reply then from this point onwards they would be responsible for the continuation of the war.[12] The Estonian delegation in Paris discussed the proposed peace negotiations with the Allied delegations. None were really in a position to advise the Estonians not to make peace. The French and American delegations did stress that they themselves had no intention of making peace with or recognising the Bolsheviks, especially given the promising position of Denikin, now the focus of anti-Bolshevik military hopes. For the British delegation, E H Carr told them that he had insufficient information on British policy, and couldn't give them any useful indication about what the British attitude to the negotiations would be. The Baltic delegations made one last ditch attempt to press for Allied recognition at the Peace Conference, in the joint letter to the President of the Peace Conference of 6 September 1919, which made clear that they were, otherwise, intending now to make peace with the Soviet government.

In addition an informal meeting of Estonian, Latvian and Lithuanian representatives took place at Riga on 10 September, and another including Finnish representatives in Tallinn on 14 September, to discuss what the position of the three Baltic States ought to be towards the Soviet government. By this time all three governments had received communications from the Soviet government along the same lines as that received initially by the Estonians. The Tallinn conference decided that the Baltic governments would adopt a common front in their negotiations with the Bolsheviks, work out the specific conditions to be demanded by each state in advance, and keep the Allies informed at all stages of the negotiations. After consultation with their governments the delegates would reconvene for a conference in Tartu on 29 September. At this conference it was proposed that negotiations between all parties should open in Tartu some time in October. The Soviet government were agreeable to this, but a change of government in Lithuania and the presence of the Inter-Allied Commission for the evacuation of the Germans in Riga meant that the peace negotiations were delayed for a time, and when they did go ahead, the Estonian, Latvian and Lithuanian governments conducted them separately.

An Estonian delegation in which Ants Piip played a leading role began negotiations at Tartu on 5 December 1919, and concluded the Treaty of Tartu on 2 February 1920. According to the terms of the treaty, Soviet Russia recognised the independence of Estonia on the basis of 'the right of all peoples to self-determination, to the point of seceding completely from the State of which they form part'. They renounced Russia's rights of sovereignty over the Estonian people and territory 'voluntarily and forever'.[13] This was less than Piip had hoped for – his position had been that the collapse of the Russian Empire had resulted in the independence of a number of component parts, including Russia and Estonia, which were equals and were in a position to recognise each other. He did not admit the right of Soviet Russia to renounce sovereignty over Estonia. *According to our theory, which I defended very strenuously at the Tartu conference against the*

Russian delegation, we held that Russia fell into pieces and not that we separated ourselves. We never could agree on this point. We said we were equally qualified heirs with Great Russia ... the Soviet delegation said the Baltic States were like grown-up, marriageable daughters whom they would marry off, and to whom they were willing to give a bridal dowry.[14]

Meierovics telegraphed to the Soviet and Estonian delegations at Tartu that the Latvian government wanted to be associ-

> 'We said we were equally qualified heirs with Great Russia ... the Soviet delegation said the Baltic States were like grown-up, marriageable daughters whom they would marry off, and to whom they were willing to give a bridal dowry.'
> **ANTS PIIP**

ated with the peace talks, but the message did not reach the delegates until after the Treaty of Tartu had been signed. A Latvian peace delegation was sent to Moscow in April 1920, and the negotiations were eventually concluded in Riga on 11 August 1920. The same formula regarding recognition and self-determination that had been applied for Estonia in the Treaty of Tartu was used in the Treaty of Riga.[15]

Negotiations between the Soviet and Lithuanian governments began in May 1920. As these negotiations took place in the context of the Polish-Soviet War, some of the territorial claims accepted by the Soviet government came with strings attached – the recognition of the Lithuanian claim to Vilnius, for example, was initially to be granted on condition that the Lithuanians undertake a military alliance with the Soviet Union against Poland. They later settled for the transit of Soviet troops through Lithuanian territory. Otherwise the formula used was again similar to that used in the treaties with Estonia and Latvia. The Lithuanian delegation argued for recognition of Lithuanian independence on the basis of its continuity as an independent state, but they were forced to settle for the weaker formula of independence on the basis of the self-determination of nations. The treaty was signed in Moscow on 12 July 1920.[16]

The Soviet government, then, was the first power to offer *de jure* recognition to the Baltic States. Estonia received *de jure* recognition from the Finnish government in July 1920, and from the Polish Government in December 1920. At the beginning of 1921 when a change of cabinet in France brought Aristide Briand, known to be sympathetic to the cause of Baltic independence, to power, Meierovics made a trip to the Allied capitals to press for recognition of Baltic independence. He met Briand in Paris, and managed to persuade him to put the question of recognition of Estonia, Latvia and Lithuania on the agenda of the next meeting of the Supreme Council. When the Council met on 26 January, the decision to accord *de jure* recognition to both Estonia and Latvia was carried (despite an embarrassing difference of opinion between the British delegates Lloyd George and Lord Curzon).[17] In the wake of this decision, the consuls of Sweden, Norway and Denmark visited Ants Piip at the Estonian Foreign Office on 5 February 1921 to extend their countries' *de jure* recognition. Finland and Poland gave Latvia *de jure* recognition on the day of the Supreme Council decision, and German, Norwegian, Swedish and Danish recognition were all accorded during February. The German government finally recognised Estonia in July 1921.

The change in Allied attitudes to Estonian and Latvian recognition had been brought about in some part by their establishment of diplomatic relations with the Soviet Union. But it undoubtedly had much to do with the definitive defeat, by the beginning of 1920, of the anti-Bolshevik forces in the Russian Civil War. Without the prospect of a restored, anti-Bolshevik Russia laying claim to the territories of its former empire, there was no logical reason not to recognise the stable independent states on the eastern shore of the Baltic. Both Estonia and Latvia were admitted to the League of Nations on 22 September 1921.

The Supreme Council did not choose to extend recognition to the Lithuanian government at its meeting in January 1921. The British Government had accorded Lithuania *de facto* recognition in September 1919, but was unwilling to go further while there was uncertainty about Lithuania's frontiers. The French government were even less forthcoming. The settlement of the dispute over Vilnius, although it did not go in Lithuania's favour, improved the prospects for Lithuanian recognition. The Conference of Ambassadors in Paris decided to grant the Lithuanian government *de jure* recognition on 30 June 1922. The United States government formally recognised all three Baltic States in July 1922, despite the fact that up to this point it had refused to accord them even *de facto* recognition.

Augustinas Voldemaras (1883–1942).

III
The Legacy

9

The Inter-war Legacy

By the autumn of 1919 all three diplomats had returned to the Baltic region to take up positions in their respective governments. Ants Piip returned to work in the Ministry of Foreign Affairs in Tallinn under the governments of Otto Strandman, a former lawyer and member of Tallinn City Council, who was Prime Minister between May and November 1919, and Jaan Tönisson, who was Prime Minister from November 1919 until July 1920. Piip was closely involved in the peace negotiations with the Soviet government. He was also invited to take up a position as Professor of International Law at the University of Tartu, which he held until 1940. Zigfrīds Meierovics resumed his duties as Foreign Minister in the government of Kārlis Ulmanis, and also began the process of working for peace with the Soviet Union. The return of Augustinas Voldemaras to Kaunas sparked more controversy – perhaps unsurprisingly considering the circumstances in which he had left Lithuania nine months earlier. Although he had retained the position of Minister for Foreign Affairs while in Paris, Voldemaras was unhappy with the lack of degree of personal power Sleževičius exercised as Prime

Minister, and with the direction of policy towards peace with the Bolsheviks. Martinas Yčas, who returned to Kaunas with Voldemaras, accused Sleževičius of governing without consultation with the Taryba.

'Professor Voldemaras and I, as members of the Taryba, delivered a sharp protest to the Chairman of the Taryba, S. Silingas, against such a passive position. We pointed out that the functions of the Taryba were clearly laid out in the provisional constitution and that it could not dissolve itself or suspend its activity until the meeting of the Constituent Assembly. Silingas could not but agree with the protest ... Prime Minister Sleževičius declared he would resign if the Taryba were convoked against his wish.

'The Taryba did not concede this, and Sleževičius's cabinet fell. The President [Antanas Smetona] invited the engineer Galvanauskas, former secretary of the Lithuanian Peace Delegation, who had just returned from abroad, to form a new cabinet.' Sleževičius explained the incident somewhat differently, in a letter to Jurgis Šaulys. 'You see, the Paris delegation (Yčas, Voldemaras, and later Galvanauskas), having returned to Kaunas, decided to take the government into its own hands. Intrigues began. Smetona, as you know, lends himself easily to just such things. So they finally forced the cabinet to resign.'[1]

Voldemaras was again appointed Foreign Minister in the new cabinet, and quickly reoriented Lithuanian policy towards the Allied Powers, concentrating his resources on missions in their capitals, and even returning to Paris briefly, leaving Petras Klimas as acting Minister of Foreign Affairs in Kaunas. *Now the positive work begins*, he wrote to Šaulys, *Our ministry is looking more toward opening and extending commercial ties with foreign countries, first of all with the great states, whence stems our political future.*[2] Peace negotiations with Soviet Russia were a necessity, however. Although Voldemaras began these negotiations, by the time the peace was agreed he was no longer in office.

The removal of German troops from the Baltic region, peace with the Soviet Union, and the eventual recognition internationally of their independent status brought some stability to the internal political and economic situation of the Baltic States. All three adopted single-chamber parliaments, elected by proportional representation – the Riigikögu in Estonia, the Saeima in Latvia, and the Seimas in Lithuania. Political parties proliferated, and government tended to be in the hands of coalitions led by the parties representing agricultural interests – the Farmers' Union in Latvia for example – or by the socialist parties, such as the Estonian Labour Party, of which Ants Piip was a member. As might be expected, there was a very high turnover of governments. In Latvia, 39 different parties were represented in parliament between 1922 and 1934. The average life of coalitions in each country could be measured in months, rather than years.[3] However, this was also true in many Western European countries, including France, at this time. Despite the instability of the coalitions, key parties and key figures were consistently involved – Konstantin Päts and Jaan Tönisson in Estonia, Kārlis Ulmanis in Latvia, Sleževičius and Galvanauskas in Lithuania. This added to a sense of continuity. Ants Piip served as Foreign Minister on five separate occasions between

> 'Now the positive work begins. Our ministry is looking more toward opening and extending commercial ties with foreign countries, first of all with the great states, whence stems our political future.'
>
> **AUGUSTINAS VOLDEMARAS**

Europe 1923

FINLAND

Petrograd (St Petersburg)

Tallinn
ESTONIA

Riga
LATVIA

LITHUANIA

Moscow

Vilnius

Königsberg
EAST
PRUSSIA

UNION OF SOVIET
SOCIALIST REPUBLICS

Warsaw
Brest-Litovsk

POLAND

Kiev

AKIA

Budapest

ARY

Odessa

ROMANIA

Black Sea

Belgrade
Bucharest

LAVIA

BULGARIA
Sofia

Istanbul

NIA

GREECE

TURKEY

IRAQ

Athens

SYRIA

CYPRUS

1919 and 1940; he was briefly Prime Minister in a government led by the Estonian Labour Party between October and December 1920, and was State Elder for a month when that position was introduced, before his government was replaced by a coalition headed by Konstantin Päts in 1921. He also served briefly as the Estonian Ambassador to Washington in 1923–5. Zigfrīds Meierovics occupied the position of Foreign Minister continuously until his death, with the exception of a brief period in 1924. He was also Prime Minister twice, in 1921–3, and 1923–4. Augustinas Voldemaras, on the other hand, remained off the political scene for six years after the establishment of the Seimas in 1920. During this period he was Professor of History at the newly-formed University of Kaunas. He published widely in French and Lithuanian, and was an inspiring but erratic teacher – sometimes keeping students waiting for several hours, and then delivering a lecture lasting two or three hours.[4]

The rapid turnover of coalitions did not prevent the Baltic governments legislating. More than 3,000 laws were passed in Latvia in 16 years of parliamentary rule.[5] The vast majority of German-owned land was reclaimed by the government of Estonia. In Latvia the German landholders retained slightly more land but received no compensation for their losses. On the other hand, and despite the fact that all three countries had strong native ethnic majorities – 88 per cent in Estonia, 75 per cent in Latvia, and 84 per cent in Lithuania – very liberal minority legislation was introduced. In Estonia any minority community over 3,000 strong had the right to organise its own education system and cultural activities, and could raise 'culture taxes'. Perhaps this explains the surprisingly positive relationship that existed between the Baltic German populations and the newly independent governments throughout the inter-war period. Similar legislation was also put in place in Lithuania, but in reality there was much more discrimination – largely against the Polish population, as a result of persistently bad relations between the two countries over the Vilnius issue. In the economic sphere, government sponsorship helped to build up export economies based on timber and agricultural produce, for which Britain and Germany were the principal markets.

One of the most striking features of inter-war Baltic diplomacy were the attempts to build on the tradition of Baltic co-operation begun in London and Paris in 1918–19. Zigfrīds Meierovics was the guiding force behind this. In the summer of 1920 he invited representatives from Estonia, Lithuania, Finland and Poland to the first of a series of Baltic conferences at the Latvian resort of Bulduri near Riga. Meierovics believed that in order to gain the respect of their larger neighbours to the east and west (i.e. Russia and Germany), it was imperative for Latvia to reach *agreement with all our immediate neighbours to the North and South*.[6] He described this as a *vertical orientation* rather than a *horizontal orientation … which does not conform to our desires at all*.[7] The conference opened on 6 August and lasted for a month. Kaarel Pusta attended for the Estonian government, while Piip went to Paris to take over Pusta's duties there for the duration of the conference. The conference voted to adopt a treaty which prevented the signatories making agreements with third parties hostile to the other Baltic states; recommendations were also made on monetary union, communications, arbitration of disputes, and a military convention. Ratification of the treaty was sabotaged, however, by the Polish seizure of Vilnius in October that year.

The failure of attempts to establish a Baltic League

involving states other than Estonia, Latvia and Lithuania was ultimately a result of the different orientations of the powers involved. It became apparent early on that none of the Scandinavian governments except Finland would take part in negotiations – Sweden, Norway and Denmark were invited to send representatives to Bulduri, but they made a joint decision not to participate.[8] Estonia and Latvia found co-operation between themselves relatively easy – an example of this is the political and military alliance between them that was worked out by Meierovics and Piip at Valga in July 1921. This never came into force, but the Estonian and Latvian governments did conclude an alliance in October 1923. Some leading Finns, like Rudolf Holsti, were active proponents of the Baltic League idea, but the idea also generated hostility in Finnish politics, and so Finland tended to remain on the fringes of such projects, identifying increasingly with the other Scandinavian states rather than with those on the eastern Baltic. It was the Polish-Lithuanian relationship, or lack of relationship, that really blighted these projects. There was always a fear, even in Latvia, that what Piłsudski had in mind was a division of the Baltic into Polish and Finnish spheres of influence, rather than an agreement between equal states. The Lithuanian government, in turn, wanted to construct agreements that would be specifically aimed against Poland – this was the reason for their non-involvement in the 1921 and 1923 agreements. The Polish government invited Latvian, Estonian and Finnish representatives to a meeting of Foreign Ministers in Warsaw in March 1921, which culminated in the drawing up of the Warsaw Accord of 1922, a loosely-worded treaty which contained no real military alliance but paved the way for further trade and administrative agreements. Despite the reluctance of Piip and Meierovics to exclude Lithuania from any Baltic combination, it was the failure of the Finnish government to ratify this agreement that led to its ultimate failure.

Even Meierovics gradually lost patience with these attempts at 'vertical co-operation', and he began to concentrate on closer co-operation between the three Baltic States, and on improving relations with Germany and Russia. His attempts to organise a conference at Riga including Soviet representatives, Finland, the Baltic States and Poland in 1924 failed, resulting in the downfall of his cabinet. Thus chastened, he was back at the Foreign Office by the end of the year, and his policy of co-operation thereafter was less ambitious. Nonetheless, the cause of Baltic co-operation was dealt a severe blow by his premature death in August 1925. While on the way to Tukums in Kurzeme for a holiday with his children, Meierovics's chauffeur-driven car overturned, and he was killed. He was 38 years old.[9]

When Felikss Cielēns took over as Foreign Minister in 1926, he associated himself with Meierovics' policy, in a speech that he made shortly after taking up the post. 'The effort of the late Z. A. Meierovics to achieve … a political union between the Baltic States and Poland produced no results. The Warsaw treaty fell through and Mr. Meierovics realised the futility of the scheme. Our foreign policy was therefore directed towards an alliance with Estonia and Lithuania and the maintenance of cordial relations with Germany and Russia. Mr. Meierovics did not live to carry the plan into effect and it has fallen into my lot to do so.'[10]

The Treaty of Locarno of 1925 had also significantly changed the diplomatic landscape in Europe. It confirmed Germany's western frontiers as they had been agreed at Versailles, and paved the way for German entry to the League of

Nations, but made no provision for her eastern frontiers. The Lithuanian government, looking for ways to secure its position but also to keep the Vilnius question open, signed a non-aggression treaty with the Soviet Union in September 1926. Estonia, Latvia and Lithuania all signed the Baltic Entente that was eventually agreed in Geneva in September 1934, but although this allowed for collaboration in foreign affairs and mutual diplomatic support, it was a long way from the wider new Baltic Sea combination that had been envisaged earlier. In some ways it reinforced the image of the Baltic States as isolated entities between Germany and Soviet Russia.

In the Baltic States as in many other parts of Europe, the 1930s witnessed the introduction of authoritarian governments. This happened first in Lithuania in 1926, and it brought Augustinas Voldemaras back into power. In opposition to the non-aggression treaty with the Soviet Union, the Lithuanian Nationalist Party (the *Tautininkai*) and right-wing elements in the army launched a coup in December, breaking up parliament and dismissing the cabinet and the President. Antanas Smetona was installed as President, and Augustinas Voldemaras as Prime Minister and Minister for Foreign Affairs.

In Estonia a new constitution came into force in 1933 that strengthened the power of the President. Not content with this, Konstantin Päts declined to stand in presidential elections and declared a state of emergency. He took essentially dictatorial powers on 12 March 1934. Kārlis Ulmanis took very similar action in Latvia only four days later. All of these governments dealt harshly with their opponents and suppressed political parties. There were also significant consequences for national minorities in these states, as Polish and German schools were closed or restricted, and strict language requirements were introduced. Nevertheless there have been some efforts to rehabilitate the reputations of these leaders, particularly in the case of Päts and Ulmanis. It is striking that all of the individuals involved had been leaders of their countries' independence movements. There was a sense in which they were moving to protect the freedoms they had fought to establish, from fascist or paramilitary organisations like the League of Freedom Fighters in Estonia, and the Thunder Cross movement in Latvia. Ulmanis seems to have had a genuine distaste for dictatorial government and for European fascist leaders like Hitler and Mussolini – he also seems to have had broad support in Latvia. The case is more difficult to make for Päts, and even more so for Smetona and Voldemaras, who repressed serious opposition and operated strict censorship and a police state.[11] Kaarel Pusta, one of the country's foremost diplomats, lived in exile after 1935, in New York and later in Madrid. Ants Piip did not take part in national politics again until a more democratic regime was introduced in 1938, when he became a member of the new second chamber of the Riigikogu. In the intervening period he concentrated on his work at the University of Tartu, and acted as a member, and later Chairman, of the Tartu Municipal Council.

Lithuania's right-wing paramilitary organisation, *Gelezinis Vilkas* ('Iron Wolf'), was headed by Voldemaras himself. Antanas Smetona was also an honorary member, but the organisation became bound up in in-fighting between the two men, with Voldemaras attempting to use its younger, pro-fascist members to oust the president. This was a battle that Voldemaras lost when Smetona removed him from office in 1929.

Foreign policy under Voldemaras exhibited much continuity with that of the democratic government, despite his protests to the contrary. He had objected primarily to the left-wing nature of the government that had negotiated the treaty with the Soviet Union, rather than the treaty itself. He still believed that Lithuania was unique among the Baltic States because of its historic basis as a state and its lack of utility as an outlet to the Baltic. While Estonia and Latvia would always be threatened by Russia, Lithuania was better off securing good relations with both Russia and Germany. Russia, after all, was the only power that was still willing to recognise Lithuania's claim to Vilnius, and was always likely to be antagonistic towards Poland. Voldemaras 'exasperated the foreign offices of Europe' with the intransigence of his position on Vilnius.[12] There was also internal pressure to continue this policy – when Voldemaras met August Zaleski, the Polish Foreign Minister in Paris in June 1927, he was met on his return to Kaunas by a group of army officers who made it clear that they opposed any form of negotiation with the Poles.[13] Attacks on Lithuanian cultural institutions in the Vilnius region prompted the Lithuanian government to file a complaint with the Council of the League of Nations. Voldemaras and Piłsudski eventually faced each other at a secret session of the League Council in December 1927. In response to Voldmaras's long-winded explanation of the case for Lithuanian possession of Vilnius, Piłsudski 'struck the table with his open hand so hard that the water pitcher rattled, and he screamed at the Lithuanian, "I have not made the long trip from Warsaw to Geneva, M. Voldemaras, just to hear your long speech … I just want to know whether you want war or peace"'.[14] Voldemaras was obliged to concede that he wanted peace. A conference at which the Poles and Lithuanians were to negotiate was convened in Königsberg in 1928, but with no positive results. Vilnius remained in Polish hands until the Soviet invasion of Poland in 1939.

In May 1929 an unsuccessful attempt was made on Voldemaras's life. *Gelezinis Vilkas* organised demonstrations on his behalf, but in the context of rising antagonism between Voldemaras and other members of the government, Smetona dissolved the cabinet, and charged his brother-in-law, Juozas Tūbelis, with forming a new government. Voldemaras turned down the position of Foreign Minister, to the relief of his international interlocutors: *The Times* commented that there would be 'an undiplomatic sigh of satisfaction at Geneva if his intention to abandon politics is confirmed'.[15]

> 'I have not made the long trip from Warsaw to Geneva, M. Voldemaras, just to hear your long speech ... I just want to know whether you want war or peace.'
>
> PIŁSUDSKI TO VOLDEMARAS

After leaving office, Voldemaras lived under police surveillance with his family in Zarasai, an inaccessible and heavily forested lake district in north-eastern Lithuania. His supporters, who were predominantly young army officers, and were known as *Voldemarininkai*, continued to pose something of a threat to Smetona. In 1934 Voldemaras attempted an unsuccessful coup, organised by *Gelezinis Vilkas*, who flew him from Zarasai back to Kaunas. Smetona had him arrested, and he spent the years 1934–8 in prison, before going into exile in France. Smetona described Voldemaras in this period as 'a man of small stature but of great talents' who might have been 'a great political personage' but he 'lacked sincerity, was unreasonably obstinate, had blind faith in and admiration for himself, undue and unfounded suspicion of others, and lacked a sense of realities'.[16] After the fall of Voldemaras the

'Voldemaras Course' in Lithuanian foreign policy gave way to the 'Lozoraitis Concept', as the new Foreign Minister Stasys Lozoraitis strove to improve Lithuania's relationships with Poland and with the other Baltic States. However by the 1930s the nature of European diplomacy was changing rapidly. The Vilnius question seemed of limited importance in an international context, and the time for constructing regional alliances to counteract the influence of Germany and Soviet Russia was long past.

10

Loss of Independence

Neither Germany nor Soviet Russia considered the *status quo* established in 1919 acceptable in the changed international conditions of the late 1930s. The German threat in Eastern Europe impacted on the Baltic region in March 1939 when Joachim von Ribbentrop, the German Foreign Minister, gave the Lithuanian Foreign Minister Juozas Urbšys an ultimatum to return Klaipeda to the German Reich. The Lithuanian government complied two days later. Although they were heavily criticised domestically for the loss of their only real port and a significant proportion of their industrial capacity, leading members of the government were relieved, as they had feared the Germans might decide to occupy the entire country.

The Soviet government was worried about the proximity of Leningrad to its borders. In the last major war the Russians had fought, in 1914, they had controlled the eastern Baltic seaboard and Finland. In the abortive discussions that took place between Britain, France and the USSR in the spring of 1939, the Soviet Government was looking either for guarantees for the Baltic States and Finland, or for them to be assigned to a Soviet sphere of influence. This was exactly what they got from Germany in the Molotov-Ribbentrop Pact, signed on 23 August 1939. Estonia, Latvia and Finland, along with the eastern part of Poland, were assigned to a Soviet sphere of influence. A second protocol, signed a month later, assigned Lithuania to the Soviet sphere.

Almost immediately after the signature of this treaty, the Soviet government began negotiations for what were described as 'treaties of mutual assistance' with the three Baltic States. While in Moscow in September the Estonian Foreign Minister Karl Selter was presented with an ultimatum by Molotov that he sign a treaty giving the Soviet Union access to a base at the Estonian port of Paldiski, and the right to occupy several Estonian islands. Molotov pointed out that help was unlikely to be forthcoming from Britain or from Germany, and stated that the Soviet Union would occupy these bases by force if necessary. With little choice but to comply, the Estonian government sent a delegation to Moscow to conclude the treaty on 28 October. Ants Piip went as an expert in international law. Molotov and Stalin presented the Latvian Foreign Minister Vilhelms Munters with a similar treaty in early October. It was signed on 5 October, and gave the Soviets bases in Liepāja and Ventspils. Juozas Urbšys, the Lithuanian Foreign Minister, arrived in Moscow on 3 October. The treaty of mutual assistance resurrected the bargain of 1920: in return for military advantages which thoroughly compromised Lithuania's sovereignty by allowing Soviet land and air bases to be established in the country, the Lithuanian government finally regained Vilnius, which had been occupied by Soviet forces during their invasion of Poland in September 1939. Voldemaras made a brief appearance on the Lithuanian political scene during the negotiations – he arrived in Kaunas from

France in August 1939, but was arrested and shortly afterwards sent back into exile.

There was little dissent within the Baltic governments about the necessity of signing the treaties. Ants Piip clearly believed the Estonians had no choice in Moscow – attempts to resist would only bring the same result, but with more bloodshed. In Konstantin Päts's view, it was better 'to face an uncertain future with the Estonian people intact than to resort to armed resistance that would lead to the certain destruction of a significant minority of the nation'.[1] Three weeks after the signature of the treaty in Moscow, the government was reorganised, with Jüri Uluots and Ants Piip, both members of the Moscow delegation and professors at Tartu University, being installed as Prime Minister and Foreign Minister respectively. Their government's policy was aimed at avoiding further antagonising the Soviet Union, while maintaining that their country's sovereignty had not in fact been surrendered.

For a time, this position was credible: the Soviets did little to intervene in the internal affairs of the Baltic States between the autumn of 1939 and the summer of 1940, and it is not clear that Stalin and Molotov had initially intended to incorporate the Baltic States as Soviet Republics. Estonia, Latvia and Lithuania built up their trading relations with Germany in the spring of 1940 to the point where 70 per cent of their exports were going to Germany. This, and the success of the German offensive in the West, may have persuaded the Soviet government to strengthen their control over the Baltic region. In June 1940 the Estonian, Latvian and Lithuanian governments were accused of collaborating with each other in disloyalty to the Soviet Union. Soviet forces occupied all three countries, and new governments were installed. After staged demonstrations in the Baltic capitals in July, all three

states were incorporated into the Soviet Union as new socialist republics in August 1940.

In the summer of 1940 a spate of arrests and deportations took place. Presidents Päts and Ulmanis were forced to
resign and were deported into the Russian interior. President
Smetona managed to flee the country before the Soviet seizure
of power, and emigrated to the United States where he lived
until his death in 1944. Leading Baltic politicians, army officers and intellectuals including Jaan Tönisson, Johan Laidoner
and Juozas Urbšys were targeted. Augustinas Voldemaras
chose this inopportune moment to attempt another return to
Kaunas. Between 13–17 June he was in Berlin, where he seems
to have attempted to negotiate German assistance for Lithuania. On 17 June he arrived at the Lithuanian border, but he
was arrested by the Soviet authorities.[2] Ants Piip escaped
arrest in 1940, and it was not until the following summer,
when a second wave of deportations took place just before
the German invasion, that he was taken. The work of the
NKVD in the Baltic Republics had been stepped up over the
previous year, and the arrests that took place in June 1941
were conducted on the basis of pre-prepared lists. The cat-
egories of individuals set for deportation included members
of nationalist and left-wing political parties, high civil serv-
ants and individuals with foreign connections – Piip must
have been high on this list. In 1940–1 over 60,000 Estonians,
35,000 Latvians and 34,000 Lithuanians are thought to have
been deported or killed. The dates of death of many of these
individuals were not known until years later. Voldemaras died
in prison in Moscow on 16 May 1942. Ants Piip died on 1
October 1942, in a prison camp in Perm Oblast. Some depor-
tees were eventually allowed to return during the period of
Nikita Khrushchev's thaw, but few survived the years spent in

the gulag. One rare exception was Juozas Urbšys, the former Lithuanian Foreign Minister, who was released in 1954, and died in Kaunas in 1991.

The years of the Second World War had a dramatic effect on the populations of the Baltic States. In the autumn of 1939 the German Government had arranged the evacuation of as many as 65,000 Baltic Germans from Estonia and Latvia back to the Reich. While many younger Baltic Germans, encouraged by Nazi rhetoric and alienated by the stringent nationality policies of the authoritarian regimes of the 1930s, were happy to leave, for the older generation it was often a struggle. Once Von Leeb's extraordinary campaign had overrun the Baltic countries in the autumn of 1941, the region was exposed to the whims of Nazi occupation. German policy, however chaotically implemented in wartime conditions, was predicated on the possibility and desirability of Germanising the territories, and even the Balts themselves. The Jewish populations of Baltic cities were almost exterminated by the *Einsatzgruppen*, mobile killing units which accompanied the German invasion. Those who remained were herded into ghettos, many of which were later cleared and the inhabitants transferred to concentration camps. Only about 10,000 Baltic Jews, of a pre-war population of something like 250,000, are thought to have survived the war.[3] Some members of the native Baltic populations were recruited to the German army, notwithstanding routine persecution by the occupying authorities. Large numbers of ethnic German and Estonians, Latvians and Lithuanians fled to the west as the Soviet armies advanced in 1944.

Intense 'Sovietization' followed the reconquest of the Baltic by the Red Army. Between 1944 and 1952 deportations took place on an even larger scale than in 1940–1. Steps were taken to enforce the collectivisation of agriculture in the Baltic States on the same lines as the programme implemented in the rest of the Soviet Union in the 1930s. Industrialisation was also a vehicle for integration, as industrial workers were forcibly migrated to the Baltic Republics from other parts of the Soviet Union. The large native ethnic majorities that existed between the wars were drastically reduced, particularly in Latvia and Estonia. By 1979 the Latvian population of Riga had fallen to only 38.3 per cent.[4] The Baltic Republics were increasingly isolated from the West, and became an intrinsic part of the Soviet security system, with Soviet bases established on the Estonian islands, submarine bases in the Baltic ports, and surveillance stations throughout the Baltic region.

Although Britain and the USA never acknowledged the annexation of Estonia, Latvia and Lithuania, the Russian contribution to the Allied victory in the Second World War meant there was little hope for a restoration of Baltic independence in the aftermath of the war. In the increasingly bi-polar international order, there was little emphasis on national self-determination, and there was no forum like the Paris Peace Conference at which they could internationalise their cause. Nevertheless, the Baltic States were among the least fortunate in the post-war period. While other Eastern European states fell into a Soviet 'sphere', and Finland remained independent but tied to friendly relations with the Soviet Union, Estonia, Latvia and Lithuania were the only former members of the League of Nations that did not regain their inter-war independence. In Soviet historiography, individuals like Ants Piip, Zigfrīds Meierovics and Augustinas Voldemaras were dismissed as fraudulent bourgeois politicians falsely claiming to represent the people of their countries, and colluding with the representatives of Western imperial powers.[5]

The sovietization of the Baltic States did meet with internal resistance. Intensive anti-Soviet guerrilla warfare took place in all three Republics in the period 1945–52, involving as many as 100,000 individuals in Lithuania, 30,000 in Estonia and 40,000 in Latvia.[6] Partisan leaders were being reported 'killed in action' as late as the 1960s and even into the 1970s. From the 1950s onwards, during the period of Khrushchev's cultural thaw, languages, literature and song festivals provided a focus for nationalist sentiment, although this did not necessarily imply opposition to Soviet rule. In the 1970s and 1980s large-scale protests like those following the self-immolation of Romas Kalanta, a 19-year-old factory worker in Kaunas in 1972 went hand-in-hand with minor acts of individual resistance – refusing to speak Russian, or commemorating prominent figures in the Baltic national movements.

No Western government paid much attention to the fate of the Baltic Republics, however. The British Government struck a deal with the Soviet Union in 1967 whereby it took £7 million that had been deposited with the Bank of England by the Estonian and Latvian governments in 1940, and used it as compensation for Russian debts to British citizens dating back to the Bolshevik Revolution.[7] This curious conflation of governments in the territory of the former Russian Empire is reminiscent of the discussions of the Baltic Commission in 1919. Indeed, the acceptance of geopolitical realities after 1945 had deep continuities with the position taken as to the prospects of the Baltic States in 1919–20.

11

Return to Europe

The reforms introduced by Mikhail Gorbachev when he
came to power in 1985 were intended to bring about managed
change within the Soviet system which would shore up the
position of the Communist Party. *Perestroika* (restructuring)
would make the Soviet economy more efficient and competi-
tive, while *glasnost* (openness) would facilitate public input
into decision-making, inspire renewed confidence in the
regime, and build public support for Gorbachev's reforms
to counteract opposition within the leadership. In the non-
Russian Republics, new political movements often had a
nationalist or anti-Russian bent – recalling Russian domination, or focusing on the fallout from environmental disasters
caused by Soviet industrialisation. The Baltic nationalities
were well-placed to exploit these new freedoms.

However, the Baltic Republics also assumed significance as
a measure of the limits of reform. While Gorbachev became
resigned to the withdrawal of Soviet troops from Eastern
Europe, the frontier of the Soviet Union was non-negotiable.
Not only were the Estonian, Latvian and Lithuanian SSRs
strategically significant, they had the potential to develop as

economic showcases under the *perestroika* programme. This explains Gorbachev's intransigence in the face of what he described as 'nationalist excesses'. Even if Gorbachev was keen to woo public opinion in the Baltic Republics, his policy hardened the nationalist view that real reforms were only possible by breaking away from the Soviet state.

The environmental movement was a major focus for the national movement in Estonia and Latvia, with major protests on this issue in Riga in 1986 and Tallinn in 1987. Popular Fronts – coalitions of reform-minded forces – were formed in all three Baltic Republics in October 1988. As in 1917, these movements focused initially on increased autonomy rather than complete independence. The Popular Fronts were looking to agree further changes with the central authorities, rather than break away from the Soviet Union altogether. While the new political movements were often anti-Soviet, they were not necessarily anti-communist. The Popular Fronts included communists, and endorsed communist candidates in elections – what was important was to be with the national movement. However, the memory of inter-war independence, and the perceived illegality of their incorporation into the Soviet Union in 1939–40 played an increasingly important role. Commissions were set up by the Supreme Soviets in all three Republics to examine the events of 1939–40; their reports condemned the Soviet occupation and declared it null and void in November 1989. On 23 August 1989, the 50th anniversary of the Molotov-Ribbentrop pact, demonstrators formed a human chain linking hands across the Baltic Republics. The 'Baltic Way' demonstration involved over a million people and stretched for 370 miles.

As in 1917, it was the Lithuanian SSR that moved towards independence first. While all three Republics issued declarations 'about sovereignty' in 1988–9 (Estonia in November 1988, Lithuania in May 1989, and Latvia in July 1989), the Lithuanian declaration went the furthest, stating that only laws approved by the Lithuanian Supreme Soviet were valid in the Lithuanian SSR. On 11 March 1990 the Lithuanian SSR declared its independence from the Soviet Union, with the head of the Lithuanian Popular Front, Vytautas Landsbergis, becoming President. Both Estonia and Latvia adopted a more cautious policy. The Estonians looked to open negotiations with Moscow on the basis of the Tartu Treaty of 1920 in which the Soviet Union had given up the territorial rights of Russia in Estonia. They were talking about transition periods towards independence by March and May 1990. When Estonia and Latvia did declare their independence on 20 and 21 August 1991, Western acceptance was made clear by the fact that by 1 September more than 30 countries had recognised Baltic independence.

The move towards independence was also accompanied by a resurgence of Baltic co-operation. An assembly of all three Popular Fronts met in Tallinn in May 1989, promising to 'co-ordinate joint policies of the biggest popular movements of the Soviet Baltic countries and make the general public of the Soviet Union and the World at large aware of the democratic aspirations pursued by the Baltic popular movements'.[1] When Gorbachev imposed an economic blockade on Lithuania in April 1990, it was subverted by the governments of the other two Republics which channelled vital supplies through their territory. In May 1990 the presidents of Estonia, Latvia and Lithuania renewed the Baltic Entente of 1934. There was also co-operation with other Soviet Republics, including the RSFSR (Russia), whose secession from the Soviet Union ultimately cut the ground from beneath Gorbachev's feet.

The rhetoric around independence centred on the idea of a 'return to Europe'. By 2002 all three Baltic States had applied to become members of NATO and the EU, and they became members of both in 2004. Attaining membership of the EU at the same time as Poland, Hungary and the Czech Republic was a remarkable achievement considering that the Baltic States had been an integral part of the Soviet Union. In an era of increasingly assertive Russian foreign policy, the position of Estonia, Latvia and Lithuania is a complex one, and there has been debate on to what extent it is possible to speak of a new Northern Europe, and how far these states still form part of Russia's 'near abroad'.[2] Nevertheless, regional co-operation in the period following independence has operated on many levels – between the three Baltic States; within the Baltic Sea Region, and including Russia and Germany. The Council of Baltic Sea States, established in 1992, includes Norway, Sweden, Denmark and Iceland as well as Finland, Estonia, Latvia, Poland, Russia and Germany. The Baltic Assembly, established in 1991, promotes co-operation between the parliaments of the three states and discusses issues of common interest. There is a combined Baltic Battalion, Baltic Squadron and Baltic Air Surveillance Network.

The establishment of an independent regional identity and integration into European politics clearly and self-consciously built on foundations that had been laid in the interwar period. In Riga in 1934, Ants Piip had emphasised the importance of regional co-operation in preserving Baltic independence. *The law of history is the following: if the nations inhabiting the shores of the Baltic Sea are not able to create between themselves a stronger organisation, they are doomed inevitably to submit to a stronger European power of the respective period.*[3]

When they first declared their independence in 1917–18, the governments of Estonia, Latvia and Lithuania were not internationally recognised, and were not seen as viable independent entities, nor as a coherent regional unit. The absence of a powerful Russia or Germany in the aftermath of the First World War made their independence, and their representation at a forum like the Paris Peace Conference, possible. It was the military situation which ultimately won them independence and recognition – and by the same token lost these things for other leading ex-Russian territories aspiring to statehood, like the Ukraine. The diplomatic work undertaken by Ants Piip, Zigfrīds Meierovics and Augustinas Voldemaras in Paris in 1919 played an important role. They internationalised their cause, made a case for the viability of their states, and appealed not only to the current ideology but also to the pragmatism of the Allied statesmen in their rhetoric on Baltic co-operation. The historian J Hampden Jackson has described how Ants Piip and the other members of the Estonian delegation raised the Estonian cause to the same level as other, more readily recognised East European states. 'Ants Piip and C R Pusta ... with Poska, piloted the unchartered Estonian ship of state through the squalls and cross-currents of the Paris Peace Conference. The personality and grip of international law shown by these two men predisposed favourably to the Estonian people the members of the Supreme Council and of the Baltic Commission at Paris,

> 'The law of history is the following: if the nations inhabiting the shores of the Baltic Sea are not able to create between themselves a stronger organisation, they are doomed inevitably to submit to a stronger European power of the respective period.'
>
> ANTS PIIP

most of whom had never set eyes on an Estonian before. What Beneš did for Czechoslovakia, Poska, Puta and Piip did for Estonia – and not only for Estonia but for the other Baltic States as well.'[4]

Meierovics, through his collaboration with Piip and his emphasis on the potential for co-operation between small states in the Baltic region, also won recognition for his country. Hugh Rodgers, a historian of Baltic co-operation, described him in 1975: 'He was never a tribune of the people nor a popular favourite nor a dramatic orator. He played his role like the head of a liberal English government. A sense of compromise, a feeling for correctness, an absence of haughtiness, a kind and dignified bearing characterised his parliamentary leadership.'[5]

Augustinas Voldemaras tended to overestimate the weight the Allied Powers were likely to accord his country's cause, and did little to exploit the potential for including Lithuania in visions of an independent Baltic region. Nevertheless, he was the constant champion of Lithuania's demands at the Peace Conference. Henri de Chambon recalled his work as follows: 'M. Voldemaras, head of the delegation, in tireless activity, never permitting himself to be held back by any difficulty, responding immediately to each objection made, besieging the conference each day, undertaking a formidable task, assumed for a year the heavy responsibility of defending the interests of his country.'[6]

For all three Baltic states, 1919 was a crucial year for their diplomacy. It laid the foundations for their diplomatic recognition in 1921–2, and for regional co-operation in the inter-war period, and in many ways for renewed independence in 1990–1.

'The grim year of 1919 [was] spent in sparring with the

Secretariat of the Peace Conference, in arguing with its Baltic Commission, in pleading with the principal negotiators, in traversing the arguments of the Conference Politique Russe, and finally, after one of the most momentous decisions ever made by a fledgling nation, in parleying, then negotiating, then concluding armistice and peace with the Bolsheviks'.[7]

Although they would lose their independence again after only 20 years, Estonia Latvia and Lithuania never lost the legal gains they made as the result of the diplomatic work of 1919–22, or the idea that they rooted in western minds of the Baltic States as a regional entity. This was created, as much as anywhere else, in the work of Piip, Meierovics and Voldemaras in Paris in 1919.

Notes

Introduction

1. Harold Nicolson, *Peacemaking 1919* (Constable, London: 1933) pp 24–5.
2. Sir Stephen Tallents, *Man and Boy* (Faber and Faber, London: 1943) p 267.
3. Alfred Erich Senn, *The Emergence of Modern Lithuania* (Columbia University Press, New York: 1959) p 47.
4. Malbone Graham, *Diplomatic Recognition of the Border States* Vol II Estonia (University of California Press, Berkeley: 1939) p vi.
5. Hugh Rodgers, *Search for Security: A Study in Baltic Diplomacy 1920–1934* (Archon Books, Hamden, Connecticut: 1975) p 7.

1 A Brief History

1. John Hiden and Patrick Salmon, *The Baltic Nations and Europe: Estonia, Latvia and Lithuania in the Twentieth Century* (Longman, London and New York: 1994) p 13.
2. V Stanley Vardys and Romuald J Misiunas (eds), *The Baltic States in Peace and War 1917–1945* (Pennsylvania State University Press, London: 1978) p 1.

3. Marija Gimbutas, *The Balts* (Thames and Hudson, London: 1963) pp 21–2.
4. Gimbutas, *The Balts*, p 37.
5. Alfred Erich Senn, *The Great Powers, Lithuania and the Vilna Question 1920–28* (E J Brill, Leiden: 1966) p 2.

2 The Baltic Region and the Russian Empire

1. Kristina Vaicikonis, 'Augustinas Voldemaras', *Lituanus: Lithuanian Quarterly Journal of Arts and Society* 30:3 (1984).
2. Rodgers, *Search for Security*, p 15.
3. Marko Lehti, 'Sovereignty, Borders and the Construction of National Identities in Estonia and Latvia' in Lars-Folke Landgren and Maunu Häyrynen (eds), *The Dividing Line: Borders and National Peripheries* (Renvall Institute for Area and Cultural Studies: 1997) p 45.
4. David J Smith, Artis Pabriks, Aldis Purs and Thomas Lane, *The Baltic States: Estonia, Latvia and Lithuania* (Routledge, London: 2002) Latvia, p 3.
5. Hiden and Salmon, *The Baltic Nations and Europe*, p 18.
6. Lehti, 'Sovereignty, Borders and the Construction of National Identities', p 46.
7. Smith, Pabriks, Purs and Lane, *The Baltic States* Latvia, p 6.
8. Toivo U Raun, 'Estonian Social and Political Thought, 1905-February 1917' in A Ezergailis and G von Pistohlkors (eds), *Die baltischen Provinzen Russlands zwischen den Revolutionen von 1905 und 1917* (Bohlau, Koln: 1982) pp 66–7.

9. Alfonsas Eidintas, Vytautas Zalys and Alfred Erich Senn, *Lithuania in European Politics: The Years of the First Republic 1918–1940* (Macmillan, Basingstoke: 1997) pp 5–6.

10. Eidintas, Zalys and Senn, *Lithuania in European Politics* pp 6, 14. Theodore R Weeks, 'Lithuanians, Poles and the Russian Imperial Government at the Turn of the Century', *Journal of Baltic Studies* Vol XXV, No 4 (1994) p 298.

11. Weeks, 'Lithuanians, Poles and the Russian Imperial Government', pp 296–7.

12. Eidintas, Zalys and Senn, *Lithuania in European Politics*, pp 6, 12.

13. Weeks, 'Lithuanians, Poles and the Russian Imperial Government', pp 294–5.

14. Eidintas, Zalys and Senn, *Lithuania in European Politics*, p 15.

15. Raun, 'Estonian Social and Political Thought', pp 63–5.

16. Andrejs Plakans, 'Two 1905 Congresses in Latvia: a Reconsideration', *Journal of Baltic Studies* Vol 38, No 4 (December 2007) pp 401–17.

17. Eidintas, Zalys and Senn, *Lithuania in European Politics*, pp 18–19.

18. Uldis Germanis, 'The Idea of Independent Latvia and its Development in 1917' in Adolf Sprudz and Armins Rusis (eds), *Res Baltica: A Collection of Essays in Honour of the Memory of Dr. Alfred Bilmanis (1887–1948)* (A W Sijthoff, Leyden: 1968) p 29.

3 War, Revolution and Independence

1. Senn, *Emergence of Modern Lithuania*, pp 18–19.

2. Edgar Anderson, 'Through the Baltic Gate: Impact of the First World War on the Baltic Area', *Baltic Review* Vol 33 (1967) p 5.

3. Germanis, 'The Idea of Independent Latvia', pp 30–1.

4. Rodgers, *Search for Security*, pp 15–16.

5. Eidintas, Zalys and Senn, *Lithuania in European Politics*, p 21.

6. Algirdas M Budreckis, *The Lithuanians in America 1651–1975* (Oceana Publications Inc, New York: 1976) pp 21–2.

7. Germanis, 'The Idea of Independent Latvia', p 32.

8. Olavi Arens, 'The Estonian Maapäev during 1917' in Vardys and Misiunas (eds), *The Baltic States in Peace and War 1917–1945*, pp 20–1.

9. Lehti, 'Sovereignty, Borders, and the Construction of National Identities', p 48.

10. A Klive, *Latvijas brīvvalsts* (Riga: 1920) p 215, cited in Andrew Ezergailis, *The 1917 Revolution in Latvia* (Columbia University Press, New York: 1974) pp 196–7.

11. Eidintas, Zalys and Senn, *Lithuania in European Politics*, pp 29–30.

12. Eric A Sibul, 'The Origins of Estonian Diplomacy 1917–1922: the roles of Kaarel Robert Pusta, Antonius Piip and Jaan Poska', San Jose State University Masters Thesis (1989) p 27.

13. A Ezergailis, 'The Latvian Liberals and the Federative Tradition during the 1917 Revolution', *Lituanus: Lithuanian Quarterly Journal of Arts and Society* 17:3 (1971).

14. 'Notes of a Conversation with Professor Woldemar' by J Y Simpson, 5 February 1919, in The National Archives FO 608/195, hereafter TNA.

15. Interview with Ants Piip at the Estonian Foreign
    Office, 12 August 1930, cited in Graham, *Diplomatic
    Recognition of the Border States* Vol II: Estonia,
    pp 235–6.
16. Senn, *Emergence of Modern Lithuania*, p 31.
17. Senn, *Emergence of Modern Lithuania*, p 49.
18. Ronald Grigor Suny, cited in Smith, Pabriks, Purs and
    Lane, *The Baltic States*, Latvia, p 13.

4 Early Allied Contacts
 1. Zourab Avalishvili, *The Independence of Georgia
    in International Politics 1918–1921* (Headley Bros,
    London: 1940) p 143.
 2. *Foreign Relations of the United States* 1918, Russia Vol
    II, pp 815–6, hereafter *FRUS*.
 3. *FRUS* 1918, Russia Vol II, pp 815–16.
 4. Sibul, 'The Origins of Estonian Diplomacy', p 36.
 5. Esme Howard, *Theatre of Life* (Hodder and Stoughton,
    London: 1936) pp 258–9.
 6. *FRUS* 1918, Russia Vol II, pp 818–19.
 7. Sibul, 'The Origins of Estonian Diplomacy', p 44.
 8. J D Gregory, *On the Edge of Diplomacy* (Hutchinson,
    London: 1929) pp 184–6.
 9. Notes by E H Carr to Memo of the Commission on
    Baltic Affairs, 16 July 1919, TNA: FO 608/186.
10. Sibul, 'The Origins of Estonian Diplomacy', p 69.
11. Heikki Roiko-Jokela, *Ihanteita ja reaalipolitiikkaa:
    Rudolf Holstin toiminta Baltian maiden kansainvälisen
    de jure –tunnustamisen ja reunavaltioyhteistyön
    puolesta 1918–1922* (Jyväskylän yliopisto, Jyväskylä:
    1995) pp 292–3.

12. Marko Lehti, *A Baltic League as a Construct of the New Europe* (Peter Lang, Frankfurt: 1999) p 126, hereafter Lehti, *A Baltic League*.
13. Balfour to Meierovics, 11 November 1918, cited in Graham, *Diplomatic Recognition of the Border States* Vol III, Latvia, p 406.
14. *FRUS* 1918, Russia Vol II, pp 817–21, 839.
15. Senn, *Emergence of Modern Lithuania*, p 51.
16. 'Report of a Conversation with Professor Voldemar', 5 February 1919, by Rex Leeper and Lewis Namier, TNA: FO 608/195.
17. Notes by E H Carr, 11 February 1919, on 'Notes of a Conversation with Professor Woldemar' by J Y Simpson, 5 February 1919, TNA: FO 608/195.
18. 'Report of a Conversation with Professor Voldemar', 5 February 1919, by Rex Leeper and Lewis Namier, TNA: FO 608/195.

5 The Baltic Delegations in Paris

1. Senn, *The Emergence of Modern Lithuania*, pp 87–9.
2. Lord Kilmarnock in Copenhagen to the FO, 18 January 1919, TNA: FO 608/195.
3. MI6B report on 'Recent Events in Lithuania', 12 February 1919, TNA: FO 608/195.
4. Olsauskis to Balfour, 23 January 1919, TNA: FO 608/201.
5. Voldemaras to Clemenceau, 16 February 1919, cited in Henry de Chambon, *La Lithuanie Pendant la Conférence de la Paix* (V Bresle, Lille: 1931) pp 18–19.
6. Notes to No. 11656, 2 June 1919, TNA: FO 608/185.
7. Sibul, 'The Origins of Estonian Diplomacy', p 89.
8. Howard, *Theatre of Life*, p 259.

9. *Postimees*, 26 January 2008.

10. Howard, *Theatre of Life*, p 301.

11. Howard, *Theatre of Life*, p 382.

12. Howard, *Theatre of Life*, p 366.

13. Voldemaras to the Peace Conference, 24 March 1919, in Chambon, *La Lithuanie Pendant la Conférence de la Paix*, pp 21–5.

14. Senn, *Emergence of Modern Lithuania*, p 92.

15. Charles L Sullivan, 'German Freecorps in the Baltic 1918–19', *Journal of Baltic Studies* Vol VII, No 2 (1976) p 127.

16. Memorandum by the Estonian Delegation, 17 January 1919, TNA: FO 608/182.

17. Dr O Kallas to Dr A Piip, 6 January 1919, TNA: FO 608/182.

18. Ed Virza, *Z. A. Meierovics, Latvijas pirmā ārlietu ministra* (Riga: 1935) p 420.

19. Memorandum by the Estonian Delegation, 17 January 1919, TNA: FO 608/182.

20. Memorandum by Sir Esme Howard, 18 January 1919, TNA: FO 608/182; Appeal by Latvian Delegation, 13 February 1919, TNA: FO 608/183, and Z Meierovics to Lord R Cecil, 19 March 1919 TNA: FO 608/183.

21. Balfour to Curzon in No. 2252, TNA: FO 608/183.

22. Herbert Hoover, *The Hoover Memoirs* 3 vols (Hollis & Carter, London: 1952) Vol I, p 411.

23. J W Headlam-Morley, *A Memoir of the Paris Peace Conference, 1919* (Methuen, London: 1972) p 6.

24. Winston Churchill, *The World Crisis: The Aftermath* (Thornton Butterworth, London: 1929) p 169.

25. *FRUS, 1919*, Russia pp 300, 361, 369.

26. Paul Mantoux, *The Deliberations of the Council of Four (March 24 – June 28 1919): From the Delivery of the Peace Terms to the Signing of the Treaty of Versailles* (Princeton University Press, Princeton: 1992) Vol II, p 194.

27. Howard, *Theatre of Life*, p 277.

28. 'Copie de la note remise par la Conférence Russe à la Conférence de la Paix', TNA: FO 608/184. See also Memorandum by the Russian Political Conference, cited in Graham, *Diplomatic Recognition of the Border States* Vol II Estonia, pp 259–60.

29. Russian Political Conference Memorandum to Clemenceau, 24 May 1919, cited in Graham, *Diplomatic Recognition of the Border States* Vol III Latvia, p 412.

30. Kay Lundgreen-Neilsen's *The Polish Problem at the Paris Peace Conference: a study of the policies of the Great Powers and the Poles, 1918–19* (Odense University Press, Odense: 1979) gives a full account of the divisions in the Polish delegation over the extent of Poland's borders.

31. For example James Simpson to William Tyrrell, 7 June 1919, TNA: FO 371/4380.

32. Voldemaras to Clemenceau, 16 February 1919, in Chambon, *Lithuanie Pendant la Conférence de la Paix*, p 18.

6 Baltic Co-operation in Paris

1. Lehti, *A Baltic League*, pp 120–7.

2. Conference de la Paix 1919–1920, *Recueil des Actes de la Conférence* Part IV, C (2) (Imprimerie Nationale, Paris: 1923) pp 143–4, hereafter *Recueil des Actes*.

3. Letter from the Delegates of the Baltic States to the President of the Peace Conference, 6 September 1919, in *Recueil des Actes* Part 4, C (7) p 212.

4. Memorandum by Jaan Poska, 28 March 1919, and letter from Estonian Delegation 1 April 1919, TNA: FO 608/184.

5. 'Communication from the Lettish Delegation relative to the situation of that government with reference to Russia', 24 March 1919, in Graham, *Diplomatic Recognition of the Border States* Vol III Latvia, pp 462–3, and letter from Latvian Delegation, 1 April 1919 TNA: FO 608/184.

6. Latvian note to the Peace Conference of Paris Regarding the Proposed Recognition of the Government of Admiral Kolchak, by Z A Meierovics, 30 May 1919, in Graham, *Diplomatic Recognition of the Border States* Vol III Latvia, pp 469–70.

7. Howard, *Theatre of Life*, p 260.

8. Lehti, *A Baltic League*, pp 129–31.

9. Tönisson's speech to the Maapäev, cited in Arens, 'The Estonian Maapäev during 1917', pp 24–5.

10. Lehti, 'Sovereignty, Borders, and the Construction of National Identities', pp 49–50.

11. Lehti, *A Baltic League*, p 134.

12. Rodgers, *Search for Security*, p 14.

13. Notes of a conversation with Mr Woldemar by J Y Simpson, 5 February 1919, TNA: FO 608/195.

14. *FRUS* 1918, Russia Vol II, pp 815–16.

15. Memoranda by Sir Esme Howard, 29 July 1918, TNA: FO 371/3358, and 3 December 1918, TNA: FO 371/3349.

16. Memorandum by the Estonian Delegation, 17 January 1919, TNA: FO 608/182.

17. Graham, *Diplomatic Recognition of the Border States* Vol II Estonia, p 262.
18. *FRUS* 1919, The Paris Peace Conference, Vol IV, p 688.
19. *FRUS* 1919, The Paris Peace Conference, Vol IV, pp 692–3

7 The Baltic Commissions

1. Paul Mantoux, *The Deliberations of the Council of Four* (March 24–June 28 1919) (Princeton University Press, Princeton: 1992) p 258.
2. Mantoux, *Deliberations of the Council of Four*, p 399; and *Recueil des Actes* Part 4, C (7) p 1.
3. Minutes of a Meeting of the Council of Foreign Ministers, 9 May 1919, in Michael Dockrill (ed), *British Documents on Foreign Affairs: Reports and Papers from the Foreign Office Confidential Print* Part II Series I (University Publications of America, Frederick, Maryland: 1989–91) Vol 3, p 208.
4. Report of the Commission to Consider the Baltic Question, TNA: FO 608/186.
5. *FRUS* 1919, The Paris Peace Conference, Vol IV, p 755.
6. *Recueil des Actes* Part 4, C (7) pp 6–7.
7. *Recueil des Actes* Part 4, C (7) pp 4–14.
8. *Recueil des Actes* Part 4, C (7) pp 30–2.
9. *Recueil des Actes* Part 4, C (7) p 37.
10. *Recueil des Actes* Part 4, C (7) pp 41–4.
11. *Recueil des Actes* Part 4, C (7) p 50.
12. *Recueil des Actes* Part 4, C (7) pp 50–1.
13. *Recueil des Actes* Part 4, C (7) pp 51–2.
14. *Recueil des Actes* Part 4, C (7) pp 54–64.
15. *Recueil des Actes* Part 4, C (7) pp 68–70.
16. *Recueil des Actes* Part 4, C (7) pp 74–5.

17. *Recueil des Actes* Part 4, C (7) pp 7–71.

18. *Recueil des Actes* Part 4, C (7) p 106.

19. Senn, *Emergence of Modern Lithuania*, pp 199–20.

20. *Recueil des Actes* Part 4, C (7) pp 144–8.

21. *Recueil des Actes* Part 4, C (7) pp 88–91.

22. Howard, *Theatre of Life*, p 381.

23. *Recueil des Actes* Part 4, C (7) pp 66–8.

24. *Recueil des Actes* Part 4, C (7) pp 91–6.

25. Hubert Gough to Field Marshal Sir Henry Wilson, 15 June 1919, HHW/2/49/1, Imperial War Museum.

26. Senn, *Emergence of Modern Lithuania*, p 98.

27. Wilson to Gough, 21 June 1919, HHW2/49/2.

28. H De La Poer Gough, *Soldiering On* (Arthur Baker, London: 1954) pp 190–202.

29. Gough to Wilson, 8 September 1919, HHW2/49/6.

30. *Recueil des Actes* Part 4, C (7) pp 15–23.

31. *Recueil des Actes* Part 4, C (7) pp 79–81.

32. Senn, *Emergence of Modern Lithuania*, p 133.

33. *Recueil des Actes* Part 4, C (7) pp 183, 219.

34. *Recueil des Actes* Part 4, C (7) pp 120–1, 131–2.

35. *Recueil des Actes* Part 4, C (7) pp 134–5.

36. *Recueil des Actes* Part 4, C (7) p 161.

37. *Recueil des Actes* Part 4, C (7) pp 209–10, 220–1.

38. *Recueil des Actes* Part 4, C (7) p 226.

39. Notes by E H Carr in file no. 15402, TNA: FO 608/186.

40. Esme Howard, *Theatre of Life*, p 361.

41. Esme Howard, *Theatre of Life*, pp 296–7.

42. Senn, *Emergence of Modern Lithuania*, pp 171, 178.

43. Jekabs Ligotnu, *Zigfrīds Meierovics: mūžs, darbs, liktens* (Valters un Rapa, Riga: 2001) p 85.

8 Settlement of Territorial Questions and Recognition

1. Charles L Sullivan, 'The 1919 German Campaign in the Baltic: The Final Phase' in Vardys and Misiunas (eds), *The Baltic States in Peace and War 1917–1945*, pp 31–42.

2. *Recueil des Actes* Part 4, C (7) pp 239–49.

3. Senn, *The Great Powers, Lithuania and the Vilna Question*, pp 2–3.

4. Notes of a Conversation with Professor Woldemar, by James Young Simpson, 5 February 1919, TNA: FO 371/4377.

5. *Recueil des Actes* Part 4, C (7) p 18.

6. Eidintas, Zalys and Senn, *Lithuania in European Politics*, p 87.

7. *Recueil des Actes* Part 4, C (7) pp 201–2, 230.

8. Eidintas, Zalys and Senn, *Lithuania in European Politics*, p 91.

9. Eidintas, Zalys and Senn, *Lithuania in European Politics*, pp 85–99.

10. Tallents, *Man and Boy*, pp 371–9.

11. Zenonas Butkas, 'Great Britain's mediation in establishing the Lithuanian-Latvian frontier, 1920–21', *Journal of Baltic Studies* XXIV (4) (1993) pp 359–68. Charlotte Alston, 'James Young Simpson and the Latvian-Lithuanian border settlement 1920–21: the papers in the archive of the Royal Scottish Geographical Society' *Scottish Geographical Journal* 118 (2) (2002) pp 87–100.

12. Senn, *Emergence of Modern Lithuania*, p 152.

13. Graham, *Diplomatic Recognition of the Border States* Vol II Estonia, pp 283–4.

14. Ants Piip, *Estonia's Political and Economic Development* (Brookings School Lectures, No. 1, February 12 1925),

pp 9–10, cited in Graham, *Diplomatic Recognition of the Border States* Vol II Estonia, p 336.

15. Graham, *Diplomatic Recognition of the Border States* Vol III Latvia, pp 437–8.
16. Eidintas, Zalys and Senn, *Lithuania in European Politics*, pp 67–70.
17. Graham, *Diplomatic Recognition of the Border States* Vol II Estonia, pp 289–90.

9 The Inter-war Legacy

1. Senn, *Emergence of Modern Lithuania*, pp 171–2.
2. Senn, *Emergence of Modern Lithuania*, p 177.
3. Hiden and Salmon, *The Baltic Nations and Europe*, p 50.
4. Vaicikonis, *Augustinas Voldemaras*, available at http://www.lituanus.org/1984_3/84_3_06.htm.
5. Hiden and Salmon, *The Baltic Nations and Europe*, p 50.
6. Rodgers, *Search for Security*, p 16.
7. Rodgers, *Search for Security*, p 22.
8. Lehti, *A Baltic League*, p 263.
9. *The Times*, 24 August 1925, p 12.
10. Rodgers, *Search for Security*, p 58.
11. Hiden and Salmon, *The Baltic Nations and Europe*, pp 51–8.
12. Senn, *The Great Powers*, p 224.
13. Eidintas, Zalys and Senn, *Lithuania in European Politics*, pp 140–2.
14. Alfred Erich Senn, *The Great Powers, Lithuania and the Vilna Question 1920–1928* (E J Brill, Leiden: 1966) p 197.

15. Senn, *The Great Powers, Lithuania and the Vilna Question*, p 232.
16. Alfred Erich Senn, *Lithuania 1940: Revolution from Above (On the Boundary of Two Worlds: Identity, Freedom and Moral Imagination in the Baltics)* (Rodopi, Amsterdam and New York: 2007) p 29.

10 Loss of Independence

1. Toivo Raun, *Estonia and the Estonians* (Hoover Institution Press, Stanford, California: 2002) p 142.
2. Senn, *Lithuania 1940*, pp 109, 140.
3. Romuald Misiunas and Rein Taagepera, *The Baltic States: Years of Dependence 1940–1990* (University of California Press, Berkeley and Los Angeles: 1993) p 64.
4. Hiden and Salmon, *The Baltic Nations and Europe*, p 131.
5. For example H Talvar, *The Foreign Policy of Estonia 1918–21* (Perioodika, Tallinn: 1978).
6. Romuald and Taagepera, *The Baltic States*, p 86.
7. Hiden and Salmon, *The Baltic Nations and Europe*, p 137.

11 Return to Europe

1. Hiden and Salmon, *The Baltic Nations and Europe*, p 153.
2. David J Smith, 'Nordic near abroad or new Northern Europe? Perspectives on post-Cold War regional co-operation in the Baltic Sea Area' in Marko Lehti and David J. Smith (eds), *Post Cold War Identity Politics: Northern and Baltic Experiences* (Frank Cass, London: 2003).
3. Cited in Lehti, *A Baltic League*, p 11.

4. J Hampden Jackson, *Estonia* (London: 1940) p 151.
5. Rodgers, *Search for Security*, p 116.
6. Henri de Chambon, *La Lithuanie Pendant la Conférence de la Paix*, pp 31–2.
7. Graham, *Diplomatic Recognition of the Border States* Vol II Estonia, p 303.

Chronology

(Before 1918 Russia used the Julian calendar, which was 13 days behind the western Gregorian calendar at the beginning of the 20th century. All dates for events taking place in the Russian Empire before this date are listed according to the Julian calendar).

YEAR	AGE	THE LIVES AND THE LAND
1883		16 Apr: Birth of Augustinas Voldemaras.
1884	1/-/-	28 Feb: Birth of Ants Piip.
1887	4/3/-	5 Feb: Birth of Zigfrīds Meierovics.
1905	22/21/8	Jan–Dec: Revolutionary year in Russia and the Baltic provinces.
1906	23/22/19	5 May: Opening of first Russian Duma.
1907	24/23/20	June: Stolypin's electoral reforms limit Baltic participation in Duma.
1908	25/24/21	Piip founds and is president of the Estonian Association of Saaremaa (to 1912).
1910	27/26/23	Voldemaras graduates from University of St Petersburg.

YEAR	HISTORY	CULTURE
1883	British decide to evacuate the Sudan.	Nietzsche, *Thus Spake Zarathustra*.
1884	Berlin Conference of 14 nations on African affairs.	Mark Twain, *Huckleberry Finn*.
1887	Queen Victoria's Golden Jubilee.	Arthur Conan Doyle, *A Study in Scarlet*.
1905	Anglo-Japanese alliance renewed for ten years.	E M Forster, *Where Angels Fear to Tread*.
1906	Major earthquake in San Francisco USA kills over 1,000.	Foundation of *Everyman's Library* by Edward Dent.
1907	Peace Conference held in The Hague.	Joseph Conrad, *The Secret Agent*.
1908	Edward VII and Tsar Nicholas II meet at Reval.	Kenneth Grahame, *The Wind in the Willows*.
1910	King Edward VII dies; succeeded by George V.	H G Wells, *The History of Mr Polly*.

YEAR	AGE	THE LIVES AND THE LAND
1913	30/29/26	Piip graduates from University of St Petersburg; he takes up a research scholarship at the University, along with work for the Russian government.
1914	31/30/27	1 Aug: Germany declares war on Russia. Russians defeated at Battles of Tannenberg and Masurian Lakes
1915	32/31/28	Voldemaras joins faculty of St Petersburg University as Lecturer in History.
		Latvian Rifle Units formed in support of Russia; Meierovics is on the organising committee.
		19 Sep: German army enters Vilnius.
		Nov: Latvian and Lithuanian territories administered as *Land Oberost*, under German occupation (Riga not taken until 1917).
1917	34/33/30	24 Feb: Outbreak of revolution in Petrograd.
		Meierovics joins Foreign Relations Department of Latvian National
		Council in Petrograd.
		Mar: Voldemaras attends Brest-Litovsk negotiations.
		30 Mar: Administrative unification of Estonian territory.
		8–11 Sep: Piip, Voldemaras and Meierovics all attend the Nationalities Congress in Kiev.
		Congress in Kiev
		18–22 Sep: Vilnius Conference elects a 20-member Taryba to act as Lithuanian people's authority.
		25 Oct: Bolshevik seizure of power in Petrograd.

YEAR	HISTORY	CULTURE
1913	Bulgarians renew Turkish War. Second Balkan war breaks out.	Thomas Mann, *Death in Venice.* Marcel Proust, *Du côté de chez Swann.*
1914	Outbreak of First World War: Battles of Mons, the Marne and First Ypres: trench warfare on the Western Front.	James Joyce, *Dubliners.* Film: Charlie Chaplin in *Making a Living.*
1915	First World War: Battles of Neuve Chapelle and Loos. The 'Shells Scandal'. Gallipoli campaign. Germans sink the British liner *Lusitania,* killing 1,198.	Joseph Conrad, *Victory.* John Buchan, *The Thirty-Nine Steps.* Ezra Pound, *Cathay.* Film: *The Birth of a Nation.*
1917	First World War: Battle of Passchendaele (Third Ypres). British and Commonwealth forces take Jerusalem. USA declares war on Germany. Balfour Declaration favouring the establishment of a national home for the Jewish People in Palestine. China declares war on Germany and Russia. German and Russian delegates sign armistice at Brest-Litovsk.	P G Wodehouse, *The Man With Two Left Feet.* T S Eliot, *Prufrock and Other Observations.* Film: *Easy Street.*

YEAR	AGE	THE LIVES AND THE LAND
1918	35/34/31	16 Feb: Lithuanian declaration of independence.
		24 Feb: Estonian declaration of independence.
		3 Mar: Germany and Soviet Russia sign Treaty of Brest-Litovsk.
		20 Mar: British and French recognition of Estonian Constitutional Assembly.
		Voldemaras joins the Taryba.
		Nov: Meierovics becomes Latvian Foreign Minister; Voldemaras becomes Prime Minister of Lithuania.
		11 Nov: British recognition of Latvian Provisional Government.
		18 Nov: Latvian declaration of independence.
		22 Nov: Soviet forces invade Estonia.
		20–21 Dec: Voldemaras, together with Martynas Y as and Antanas Smetona flee Vilnius; Voldemaras goes to Berlin and then Scandinavia, London and Paris (in 1919) to solicit Allied support for independence.

YEAR	HISTORY	CULTURE
1918	First World War:	Alexander Blok, *The Twelve.*
	German Spring offensives on Western Front fail.	Gerald Manley Hopkins, *Poems.*
	Romania signs Peace of Bucharest with Germany and Austria-Hungary.	Luigi Pirandello, *Six Characters in Search of an Author.*
	Ex-Tsar Nicholas II and family executed.	
	Allied offensives on Western Front have German army in full retreat.	
	Armistice signed between Allies and Germany; German Fleet surrenders.	
	Kaiser Wilhelm II of German abdicates.	

YEAR	AGE	THE LIVES AND THE LAND
1919	36/35/32	Jan: Soviet occupation of Vilnius and Riga.
		Paris Peace Conference opens.
		Feb: Estonian forces clear Estonia of Bolshevik troops.
		Apr: German coup in Liepāja sees German Baltic control of Latvia.
		19 Apr: Polish troops seize Vilnius.
		May: Balfour's Commission on Baltic Affairs meets (to Sep); Council of Four Commission on Baltic Affairs meets.
		21 Jun–3 Jul: Battle of Cēsis; Estonian and Latvian forces defeat Germans.
		28 Jun: Signing of Treaty of Versailles.
		6 Sep: Memorandum from Estonian, Latvian and Lithuanian delegations to Peace Conference requests decision on their independence.
		Piip becomes Foreign Minister of Estonia under Otto Strandman. He also becomes Professor of International Law at the University of Tartu.
		Meierovics resumes his duties as Foreign Minister in the government of Kārlis Ulmanis.
		The Lithuanian Sleževičius cabinet falls. Voldemaras is appointed Foreign Minister in the new government.
		5 Nov: Inter-Allied Commission for evacuation of German troops in Baltic
		States (to 16 Jan 1920).

YEAR	HISTORY	CULTURE
1919	Communist Revolt in Berlin. Benito Mussolini founds fascist movement in Italy. Irish War of Independence begins. US Senate votes against ratification of Versailles Treaty, leaving the USA outside the League of Nations.	Bauhaus movement founded by Walter Gropius. Thomas Hardy, *Collected Poems*. George Bernard Shaw, *Heartbreak House*. Film: *The Cabinet of Dr Caligari*.

YEAR	AGE	THE LIVES AND THE LAND
1920	37/36/33	2 Feb: Treaty of Tartu (Soviet-Estonian Peace Treaty).
		12 Jul: Treaty of Moscow (Soviet-Lithuanian Peace Treaty).
		6 Aug: First Baltic Conference at Bulduri, Latvia.
		11 Aug: Treaty of Riga (Soviet-Latvian Peace Treaty).
		9 Oct: Polish General Żeligowski's seizure of Vilnius.
		Oct– Dec: Piip becomes Prime Minister and state elder of Estonia.
1921	38/37/34	26 Jan: British and French *de jure* recognition of Estonia and Latvia.
		Meierovics' first term as prime minister (to 1923). He serves a second term in 1923–4.
		Voldemaras appointed Professor of History at the University of Kaunas.
		22 Sep: Estonia and Latvia admitted to League of Nations.
1922	39/38/35	30 Jun: British and French *de jure* recognition of Lithuania.
		28 Jul: USA *de jure* recognition of Estonia, Latvia and Lithuania.

YEAR	HISTORY	CULTURE
1920	League of Nations comes into existence.	F Scott Fitzgerald, *This Side of Paradise*.
	The Hague is selected as seat of International Court of Justice.	Franz Kafka, *The Country Doctor*.
	League of Nations headquarters moved to Geneva.	Katherine Mansfield, *Bliss*.
		Rambert School of Ballet formed.
	Warren G Harding wins US Presidential election.	
	Bolsheviks win Russian Civil War.	
	Government of Ireland Act passed.	
	Adolf Hitler announces his 25-point programme in Munich.	
1921	Paris Conference of wartime Allies fixes Germany's reparation payments.	Aldous Huxley, *Chrome Yellow*.
		D H Lawrence, *Women in Love*.
	Irish Free State established.	John Dos Passos, *Three Soldiers*.
	Peace treaty signed between Russia and Germany.	Salzburg Festival established.
	State of Emergency proclaimed in Germany in the face of economic crisis.	Prokofiev, *The Love for Three Oranges*.
	Washington Naval Treaty signed.	
1922	Chanak crisis.	James Joyce, *Ulysses*.
	League of Nations council approves British mandate in Palestine.	British Broadcasting Company (later Corporation) (BBC) founded: first radio broadcasts.

YEAR	AGE	THE LIVES AND THE LAND
1923	40/39/36	9 Jan: Lithuanian seizure of Klaipeda.
		Piip is appointed Estonian Ambassador to Washington (to 1925).
		Oct: Estonian-Latvian Alliance.
1925	42/41/38	22 Aug: Death of Zigfrīds Meierovics in a car accident.
1926	43/42	Sep: Lithuania signs non-aggression treaty with the Soviet Union.
		17 Dec: Smetona/Voldemaras coup in Lithuania; Voldemaras leaves office in 1929.
1934	51/50	12 Mar: Päts coup in Estonia.
		16 Mar: Ulmanis coup in Latvia.
		6 Jun: Voldemaras attempts unsuccessful coup in Lithuania. He is imprisoned until 1938, when he goes into exile in France.
		12 Sep: Estonia, Latvia and Lithuania sign Baltic Entente.
1939	56/55	Mar: Lithuania returns Klapeida to the German Reich.
		Aug: Molotov-Ribbentrop Pact sees Estonia and Latvia (and Finland) returned to Soviet sphere of influence.
		Sep: Lithuania is returned to Soviet sphere.
		Oct: Treaties of Mutual Assistance between Baltic States and USSR.

YEAR	HISTORY	CULTURE
1923	French and Belgian troops occupy the Ruhr. The USSR formally comes into existence. Adolf Hitler's *coup d'état* (The Beer Hall Putsch) fails.	P G Wodehouse, *The Inimitable Jeeves.* George Gershwin, 'Rhapsody in Blue'.
1925	Locarno Treaty signed in London.	Film: *Battleship Potemkin.*
1926	General Strike in Great Britain. Germany is admitted into the League of Nations.	A A Milne, *Winnie the Pooh.* Ernest Hemingway, *The Sun Also Rises.*
1934	Hitler becomes *Führer* of Germany. USSR admitted to League of Nations. In USSR, Kirov is assassinated. Japan repudiates Washington treaties of 1922 and 1930.	Robert Graves, *I, Claudius.* Film: *David Copperfield.*
1939	Germans troops enter Prague. Italy invades Albania. Germany demands Danzig and Polish Corridor. Poland refuses. Japanese-Soviet clashes in Manchuria. Pact of Steel signed by Hitler and Mussolini. German invasion of Poland: Britain and France declare war. Soviets invade Finland.	James Joyce, *Finnegan's Wake.* John Steinbeck, *The Grapes of Wrath.* Films: *Gone with the Wind. Goodbye Mr Chips. The Wizard of Oz.*

YEAR	AGE	THE LIVES AND THE LAND
1940	57/56	Jun: Voldemaras attempts to re-enter Lithuania, but is arrested by the Soviet authorities.
		Aug: Incorporation of Estonia, Latvia and Lithuania into USSR.
1941	58/57	Jun: Piip is arrested by the Soviet authorities during a wave of deportations and killings of those with high rank or influence.
		16 May: Death, in prison, of Augustinas Voldemaras.
1942	-/58	1 Oct: Death, in Nyrybi prison camp, of Ants Piip.
1990		11 Mar: Lithuanian declaration of independence.
1991		20 Aug: Estonian declaration of independence.
		21 Aug: Latvian declaration of independence.
2004		All three Baltic States join NATO and the EU.

YEAR	HISTORY	CULTURE
1940	Second World War: German invasion of Western Europe. The Battle of Britain. Hungary and Romania join Axis.	Graham Greene, *The Power and the Glory*. Eugene O'Neill, *Long Days Journey into Night*. Films: *The Great Dictator. Pinocchio. Rebecca*.
1941	Second World War. Germany invades USSR Germans besiege Leningrad and Moscow. Soviets counter attack at Moscow. Japan attacks Pearl Harbor: Germany and Italy declare war on the USA.	Noel Coward, *Blithe Spirit*. Films: *Citizen Kane. Dumbo. The Maltese Falcon*.
1942	Second World War. Battle of Stalingrad.	Film: *Casablanca*.
1990	East and West Germany sign reunification treaty. GDR ceases to exist.	Martin Amis, *London Fields*. Film: *Goodfellas*.
1991	Military structure of Warsaw Pact is dissolved. The USSR officially ceases to exist.	Brett Easton Ellis, *American Psycho*. Film: *Thelma and Louise*.
2004	George W Bush re-elected US President.	Alan Bennett, *The History Boys* (play).

Bibliographical Essay

There is no published study devoted solely to the work of the Baltic delegations at the Paris Peace Conference. Malbone Graham discusses the work of the Estonian and Latvian delegations in some detail in *The Diplomatic Recognition of the Border States* (University of California Press, Berkeley: 1939), a three-volume work dealing with Finland (Vol I: 1936), Estonia (Vol II: 1939) and Latvia (Vol III: 1940). There is no equivalent volume for Lithuania. However, Alfred Erich Senn's *The Emergence of Modern Lithuania* (Greenwood Press, Westport: 1959) provides a good substitute, as it has several chapters that deal with developments in Paris in tandem with politics in Lithuania. Henry de Chambon's *La Lithuanie Pendant la Conférence de la Paix* (V Bresle, Lille: 1931) gives a very favourable account of Voldemaras's work in Paris, and reproduces some documents. A very useful masters thesis by Eric A Sibul, 'The Origins of Estonian Diplomacy 1917–1922: the roles of Kaarel Robert Pusta, Antonius Piip and Jaan Poska' (San Jose State University: 1989), discusses the work of three key Estonian diplomats, including Piip. There is also a masters thesis by Jānis J Samts, 'The Origins of Latvian Diplomacy 1917–1925: the role of Zigfrīds Anna

Meierovics' (San Jose State University: 1975), which I was unfortunately unable to consult for this study.

None of the three Baltic delegates featured in this book published their own account of this period. Ants Piip described his mission to London in 1918 in *Tormine Aasta: Ullevaade Eesti vallispoliitika esiajast 1917–1918 aastal dokumentides ja mallestusis* ['The turbulent year: an overview of preliminary Estonian foreign policy 1917–18'] (Vaba Eesti, Stockholm: 1966), but stops short before the Paris Conference. Some of the letters Zigfrīds Meierovics wrote from Paris are published in Ed Virza, *Z. A. Meierovics, Latvijas Pirma Arlietu Ministra* (Riga: 1935), which also contains biographical information. There are also two recent Latvian biographies of Meierovics: Jēkabs Līgotņu, *Zigfrīds Meierovics: mūžs, darbs, liktens* (Valters un Rapa, Riga: 2001), and Rihards Treijs, *Zigfrīds Meierovics* (Jumava, Riga: 2007). There are scraps of reminiscence by Voldemaras in Augustinas Voldemaras, *Pastabos saulelydzio valanda* ['Remarks at Twilight'] (Mintis, Vilnius: 1992), and there is a biographical article on Voldemaras by Kristina Vaicikonis in *Lituanus: Lithuanian Quarterly Journal of Arts and Society* 30:3 (1984). There are some memoirs by other key diplomatic figures of the period – a notable example is Kaarel Pusta, who wrote two volumes of memoirs – *Kehra Metsast Maailma* ['From Kehra Forest into the World'] (Kirjastus EMP, Stockholm: 1960), and *Saadiku Päevik* ['Envoy's Diary'] (Kirjastus Kultuur, New York: 1964).

There are published documents relating to the Baltic question at the Paris Peace Conference in *Foreign Relations of the United States* The Paris Peace Conference 1919, 13 vols (US Government Printing Office, Washington D.C: 1919), and in *Documents on British Foreign Policy 1919–39* First Series 1919–1925 (H.M. Stationery Office, London: 1947–1985).

The minutes of the Baltic Commission are in Conférence de la Paix 1919–20, *Recueil des Actes de la Conférence* Part IV, C (2) (Imprimerie Nationale, Paris: 1923). Minutes taken at the meetings of the Council of Four by their official translator, Paul Mantoux, are published in Arthur S. Link (ed.), *The Deliberation of the Council of Four (March 24-June 28 1919) From the Delivery of the Peace Terms to the Signing of the Treaty of Versailles* (Princeton University Press, Princeton: 1992). There are also a plethora of memoirs by Allied diplomats at the Paris Peace Conference and in the Baltic region: some of the most relevant are Esme Howard, *Theatre of Life* (Hodder and Stoughton, London: 1936), Herbert Grant Watson, *An Account of a mission to the Baltic States in the year 1919* (Waverley Press, London: 1919), and H de la Poer Gough, *Soldiering On* (Arthur Baker, London: 1954).

A detailed study of British policy in the Baltic region is Olavi Hovi, *The Baltic Area in British Policy 1918–21* (Finnish Historical Society, Helsinki: 1980). An article by Jan Arveds Trapans, 'The West and the recognition of the Baltic States 1919 and 1991: a study of the politics of the great powers' in *Journal of Baltic Studies* 25:2 (1994), compares Allied decision-making at Paris and afterwards with western policy in 1991. There are also a number of studies of Allied policy on Russia at the Peace Conference which touch on the Baltic States: John M. Thompson, *Russia, Bolshevism and the Versailles Peace* (Princeton University Press, Princeton: 1966), Keith Neilson, '"That elusive entity British policy in Russia": the impact of Russia on British Policy at the Paris Peace Conference' in Michael Dockrill and John Fisher (eds), *The Paris Peace Conference 1919: Peace Without Victory?* (Palgrave, Basingstoke: 2001); and Charlotte Alston, 'The Suggested Basis for a Russian Federation: Britain, anti-Bolshevik Russia and the Border States at the Paris Peace Conference' *History* Vol 91, No 301 (January 2006). Kay Lundgreen-Neilsen's *The Polish Problem at the Paris Peace Conference: a study of the policies of the Great Powers and the Poles 1918–19* (Odense University Press, Odense: 1979) gives a very comprehensive account of the attitudes of the Polish delegates and their impact on Lithuania.

Alfred Erich Senn's *The Great Powers, Lithuania and the Vilna Question 1920–28* (E J Brill, Leiden: 1966) takes the Vilnius question into the inter-war period. On Klaipeda, there is a study produced by the Lithuanian Information Bureau, *The Question of Memel: Diplomatic and other Documents from the Versailles Peace Conference till the Reference of the Question by the Conference of Ambassadors to the Council of the League of Nations (1919–1923)* (Eyre and Spottiswoode, London: 1934). On Baltic co-operation, there are two good studies: Hugh Rodgers, *Search for Security: A Study in Baltic Diplomacy 1920–1934* (Archon Books, Hamden, Connecticut: 1994) and Marko Lehti, *A Baltic League as a Construct of the New Europe* (Peter Lang, Frankfurt: 1999).

A number of general histories cover events in the Baltic region before, during and after 1919: Alfonsas Eidintas, Vytautas Žalys and Alfred Erich Senn, *Lithuania in European Politics: the years of the first republic 1918–40* (Macmillan, Basingstoke: 1997), John Hiden and Patrick Salmon, *The Baltic Nations and Europe: Estonia, Latvia and Lithuania in the 20th century* (Longman, London and New York: 1994). David Smith, Artis Pabriks, Aldis Purs and Thomas Lane, *The Baltic States: Estonia, Latvia and Lithuania* (Routledge, London: 2002), and Georg Von Rauch, *The Baltic States: the Years of Independence – Estonia, Latvia, Lithuania 1917–1940* (C Hurst, London: 1974) are just a few of them.

Picture Sources

The author and publishers wish to express their thanks to the following sources of illustrative material and/or permission to reproduce it. They will make proper acknowledgements in future editions in the event that any omissions have occurred.

Getty Images and Topham Picturepoint

Endpapers
The Signing of Peace in the Hall of Mirrors, Versailles, 28th June 1919 by Sir William Orpen (Imperial War Museum: Bridgeman Art Library)
Front row: Dr Johannes Bell (Germany) signing with Herr Hermann Müller leaning over him
Middle row (seated, left to right): General Tasker H Bliss, Col E M House, Mr Henry White, Mr Robert Lansing, President Woodrow Wilson (United States); M Georges Clemenceau (France); Mr David Lloyd George, Mr Andrew Bonar Law, Mr Arthur J Balfour, Viscount Milner, Mr G N Barnes (Great Britain); Prince Saionji (Japan)
Back row (left to right): M Eleftherios Venizelos (Greece);

Dr Afonso Costa (Portugal); Lord Riddell (British Press);
Sir George E Foster (Canada); M Nikola Pašić (Serbia);
M Stephen Pichon (France); Col Sir Maurice Hankey,
Mr Edwin S Montagu (Great Britain); the Maharajah of
Bikaner (India); Signor Vittorio Emanuele Orlando (Italy);
M Paul Hymans (Belgium); General Louis Botha (South
Africa); Mr W M Hughes (Australia)

Jacket images

(Front): Imperial War Museum: akg Images.
(Back): *Peace Conference at the Quai d'Orsay* by Sir William
Orpen (Imperial War Museum: akg Images).
Left to right (seated): Signor Orlando (Italy); Mr Robert
Lansing, President Woodrow Wilson (United States); M
Georges Clemenceau (France); Mr David Lloyd George, Mr
Andrew Bonar Law, Mr Arthur J Balfour (Great Britain);
Left to right (standing): M Paul Hymans (Belgium); Mr
Eleftherios Venizelos (Greece); The Emir Feisal (The
Hashemite Kingdom); Mr W F Massey (New Zealand);
General Jan Smuts (South Africa); Col E M House (United
States); General Louis Botha (South Africa); Prince Saionji
(Japan); Mr W M Hughes (Australia); Sir Robert Borden
(Canada); Mr G N Barnes (Great Britain); M Ignacy
Paderewski (Poland)

Index

Makers
of the
Modern
World

UK PUBLICATION: November 2008 to December 2010
CLASSIFICATION: Biography/History/
    International Relations
FORMAT: 198 × 128mm
EXTENT: 208pp
ILLUSTRATIONS: 6 photographs plus 4 maps
TERRITORY: world

Chronology of life in context, full index, bibliography innovative layout with sidebars